JAPANESE PAPER CRAFTING

Create 17 Paper Craft Projects & Make Your Own Beautiful Washi Paper

Michael G. LaFosse

with Richard L. Alexander and Greg Mudarri

TUTTLE PUBLISHING
Tokyo ■ Rutland, Vermont ■ Singapore

THIS BOOK IS DEDICATED WITH LOVE and special appreciation to my mother, Betty LaFosse, who encouraged me from my earliest memories to explore creative play with paper. Her sense of style and her taste for elegant design has inspired my art, and I continue to create things that we both enjoy.

DISTRIBUTED BY

North America, Latin America & Europe
Tuttle Publishing
364 Innovation Drive
North Clarendon, VT 05759-9436 U.S.A.
Tel: 1 (802) 773-8930
Fax: 1 (802) 773-6993
info@tuttlepublishing.com
www.tuttlepublishing.com

Japan
Tuttle Publishing
Yaekari Building, 3rd Floor
5-4-12 Osaki
Shinagawa-ku
Tokyo 141 0032
Tel: (81) 3 5437-0171
Fax: (81) 3 5437-0755
tuttle-sales@gol.com

Asia Pacific
Berkeley Books Pte. Ltd.
130 Joo Seng Road #06-01
Singapore 368357
Tel: (65) 6280-1330
Fax: (65) 6280-6290
inquiries@periplus.com.sg
www.periplus.com

Published by Tuttle Publishing,
an imprint of Periplus Editions (HK) Ltd.,
with editorial offices at
364 Innovation Drive,
North Clarendon, Vermont 05759 U.S.A.

Copyright © 2007 Michael G. LaFosse

Library of Congress Cataloging-in-Publication Data

LaFosse, Michael G.
  Japanese paper crafting : create 17 paper craft projects & make your own beautiful washi paper / Michael G. LaFosse, with Richard L. Alexander, and Greg Mudarri.
      p. cm.
  Includes bibliographical references.
  ISBN 978-0-8048-3848-1 (hardcover : alk. paper)
  1. Paper work. 2. Paper, Handmade. 3. Japanese paper. I. Alexander, Richard L., 1953- II. Mudarri, Greg, 1981- III. Title.
  TT870.L2337 2007
  745.54--dc22
                                    2007009553

ISBN-10: 0-8048-3848-8
ISBN-13: 978-0-8048-3848-1
ISBN-13: 978-4-8053-0924-7 (for sale in Japan only)

First edition
12 11 10 09 08 07   10 9 8 7 6 5 4 3 2 1

Printed in Singapore

Photo Credits

Michael G. LaFosse: pp. 6, 12–14 (with Greg Mudarri); 30 (step 12), 31 (steps 17, 18), 72
Greg Mudarri: pp. 6, 12–14 (with Michael G. LaFosse); 51 (Seigaiha), 56, 58, 59, 62, 63, 65, 73–75, 83–87, 101
Richard L. Alexander: All other photographs
Suminagashi patterns shown on p. 14 are by Marsha DuPre.

ACKNOWLEDGMENTS

This book would not have been possible if not for the help and input from Richard L. Alexander and Greg Mudarri, my colleagues at Origamido Studio. They helped me with the text, the photos, and even the selection, design, and testing of the projects.

First, I would like to thank Richard, my partner and co-founder of Origamido Studio, who took over many of the origami teaching duties as I worked out the diagrams and the how-to steps. He also took most of the photographs, juried the projects, and helped select the washi we used to make them.

I am also indebted to Greg Mudarri, who had recently returned from a fifteen-month stay in Japan where he was teaching English and folding paper. Greg had been studying and working with us since 2003, so he was able to jump right in and lend his expertise for the presentation of the traditional projects that I wanted to show in this book, including the *Noshi* and *Senbazuru* projects.

Finally, I would like to thank Holly Jennings and Sandra Korinchak, senior editors at Tuttle Publishing, for their patience and guidance through the process. Tuttle has been a great friend to people who love fine paper, paperfolding, and the simple elegance of traditional Japanese culture. I am grateful they gave me the opportunity to create such an interesting collection of beautiful, useful, and fun projects.

CONTENTS

CELEBRATED FRIENDSHIPS

PERSONALIZED SPACES

INTRODUCTION

Paper is my favorite art material, and some of my most favorite paper, called washi, was developed in Japan. This book is for people who also love washi and other high-quality handmade papers. At Origamido Studio we have been making paper, teaching others how to make paper by hand, and making art from fine papers for over ten years. Our students, customers, and visitors also fall in love with handmade papers, but in the beginning they seem puzzled about what they could do with it. Some even lament an addiction to fine papers—"I have stacks of wonderful, handmade papers from my travels, but I never seem to use any of it!"

This book is for paper crafters, artists, book binders, interior designers, and especially those who are interested in making their own, fine papers for arts and crafts. Beginning students at our hand papermaking classes often think they could never make their own paper. Do we expect everybody that buys this book to make their own washi-like paper? Of course not, but if so inclined, those who choose to do so will find this book an invaluable help, and all of you will be armed with more product information as you shop the paper stores.

This book is for all of you! We will show you how to enjoy your collection of washi by properly preparing it by dyeing, stiffening, and building composites. Many of the projects involve folding, others use tearing, and in some the papers are shaped and formed after moistening. In any event, the washi eventually becomes a cherished gift to a friend or loved one, or something wonderful you can enjoy in your own home or at work.

WASHI
The Magnificent "Skin" *of* Japan

The word "washi" is a combination of two Japanese words, *wa* and *shi*. Taken literally, "wa" means "peace," and "shi" means "paper." However, when used together, they have come to mean "Japanese paper," with the "wa" prefix now representing the essence of Japanese culture. Nowhere else but in Japan does a culture seem so intimately associated with fine papers. For centuries, the Japanese have embraced the exploration of paper's potential. Through this exploration, they soon realized that washi could become so many things, including clothing, lanterns, parasols, fans, windows, room screens, masks, and ceremonial decorations.

Japanese handmade papers are as beautiful, genuine, and interestingly varied as Japan itself. The patterns chosen to decorate washi are typically icons of the rich Japanese culture, landscape, and history. Like washi, Japan can show its bright colors, bustling noise, and excitement, but it can also show its softer, natural, tranquil side. From bright, silk kimono–inspired Yuzen patterns to subdued, creamy, silky whorls, washi offers a magnificent "skin" that expresses and defines Japan.

Washi is beautiful, not only on the surface but throughout: Washi's inherent character tends to shine through, even when its surface is printed, painted, or dyed. Its simple beauty belies the extraordinary effort taken to create luxurious paper with soft and supple strength.

Washi is not only beautiful but endlessly varied. Its raw materials are products of the Earth, and the three major species of plants harvested to become washi—Kozo, Mitsumata, and Gampi—are each unique, making their own inimitable contribution to the final product. Geography, topography, and local weather conditions affect these plants, which can grow quite differently in the various regions of Japan, and add to the individual personalities of the paper. These subtle differences in fine papers, like scrumptious foods and exquisite wines, do indeed enhance a civilized life. The Japanese people have long realized this and seem to respect high-quality paper perhaps a bit more than others do. So I call washi the magnificent "skin" of Japan for these reasons, but you do not have to be Japanese to appreciate, make, or use washi.

THE SPECIAL QUALITIES OF WASHI

There are countless different kinds of washi, yet there are certain recognizable qualities that set it apart from similar, western-style papers. People who encounter washi for the first time remark that it resembles cloth more than it does paper, which is probably a fair assessment due to its softness, both in look and feel. Although washi may feel soft, if made correctly it is exceedingly strong, even when wet. Its folding and tensile strength measurements are often quite high, due to the length and quality of the fibers. Its strength allows washi to be employed as a basic material for fabricating a staggering range of durable, utilitarian, and decorative items.

The overriding element that makes washi so different from other paper is that washi has a refined beauty, found even in its coarser forms. Certainly, some of this special beauty results from the care in selecting, harvesting, handling, and processing the fiber, but much comes from the skill of the papermaker. Most agree that the painstaking labor of making washi by the time-honored, traditional hand methods results in paper that reveals the inherent honesty of the materials. Soetsu Yanagi wrote, in "Washi no bi" (The Beauty of Washi), "The more beautiful it is the more difficult it is, to make trivial use of it." This is perhaps the greatest stumbling block for most people who love and purchase washi: It is too beautiful to use! Sure, you can frame it, or just keep it in drawers and look at it every so often, but washi begs to be used, and this book presents a series of delightful projects that can help you provide a suitable stage for its full appreciation.

Most people limit their thinking about using washi to simply wrapping or covering things, but with some clever techniques washi comes alive with shape and form. Even artists and craftspeople who routinely use other paper in their work enjoy the qualities of washi, yet they often avoid it because of its softness, opting for stiffer, machine-made papers. The fact is that, even though most washi wears quite well, it often must be lined, backed, or stiffened before use. This book will show you how to prepare your washi for all manner of applications. This and other essential preparation techniques will allow you to greatly expand the possibilities for using washi in your artwork or incorporating it into your surroundings to liven up and enrich your everyday life at home or at work. These techniques are not complex, but few books explain them. No wonder so much of the finest papers sit unused in the dark.

A BRIEF HISTORY OF WASHI

Scholars believe that papermaking began in China perhaps twenty-one centuries ago. It is likely that the method of making sheets of felted plant fiber became known in Japan perhaps five or six centuries later by way of trade with Korea. Certainly, papermaking methods flourished along the Silk Road trade routes to the Middle East, because paper was as useful for wrapping and separating items for sale as it was for documenting the trade transactions.

There are a staggering number of books about handmade paper and papermaking, many with instructions about how to make paper out of almost any kind of plant and recycled fibers. Those books are not about washi. Novelty papers such as those made from grasses, leaves, or weeds have their charm, but the fact is that paper as supple yet as strong and as versatile as washi is just not possible from most plants.

Making washi is somewhat akin to making fine wine. Certain types of washi are made in specific regions of Japan and often carry the names of those locations, much as fine wines may be named for the specific regions in Europe where special grapes were cultivated and unique winemaking methods were developed to process those particular grapes. Likewise, the choicest paper is skillfully made from only specific sections of carefully cultivated and harvested plants, grown in just the right regions, harvested at just the right time. The growing location is critical, because the climate dictates the plant's growth rate. The process selected for making a particular type of washi depends on the characteristics of the source materials, so it must be adjusted and refined accordingly. There are so many variables in making washi that the analogy of making fine wine is not too far off the mark.

Washi is produced by processing select bast fibers from only a few species of plants, particularly from the paper mulberry (Kozo), Mitsumata, and Gampi. These bast fibers come from the clean, nearly white, inner bark layer, also called the *phloem* (not the dark, outer bark). Under a microscope, the phloem is a complex, lacey plant tissue, a system of specialized cells including vertical sieve elements, with sieve plates located at the top and at the bottom ends of these long, skinny cells. There are also companion cells surrounding the sieve elements, thought to provide nourishment and functional control of the transportation and movements of sugar and mineral solutions. This tissue achieves a rapid transport of fluids between cells.

In contrast, on the inner side of the growing, *cambium* layer of cells, are the woody tissues, including the *xylem* and the pithy, structural core. These layers consist of stiffer, tougher, and thicker cellulose, with smaller cell walls that become woody from amorphous, polymeric deposits made by the plant. These woody tissues require a greater amount of processing, both mechanical and chemical, to make even a low-grade paper, such as that used for disposable napkins, toilet and facial tissue, or inexpensive office paper.

In the washi-making process, after the stems are cut, the bark is stripped off the wood, the bast fibers are separated from the darker bark, and the thin, green, growing layer of undifferentiated cambium is scraped away. At this stage, the fiber is often dried and shipped to processors. Processing the bast fibers by boiling in a caustic (alkaline chemical) solution digests, and allows the removal of, the cambium and companion cell protoplasm. Bits of bark, lignin, and semi-digested cambium still adhere to the mash and must be removed, often by hand with tweezers. Boiling thus makes it easier to clean, separate, and splay the remaining tubes of sieve element tissue. The fraying of these strong, long fibers in the beating process allows them to knit together in a tangled mat as the sheet of paper is being formed. This increased surface area becomes "hydrated" during beating, which allows these sites to be attracted to each other by hydrogen-bonding. The length and strength of fibers, the correct degree of hydration, and the intimacy of physical entanglement makes for strong, supple washi.

Expert papermakers were so fastidious about removing any contamination (or *chiri*) and discarded so much useful cellulose with the waste that they were able to make low-grade paper with the dregs. This is called *chirigami*. Because the best papermakers rejected more impurities, and thus more bast along with them, even their waste paper was strong. It was said that the best way to judge a papermaker was to evaluate the quality of his chirigami. Today, these papers are appreciated for the flecks and bits of impurities that lend chirigami a rustic, earthy quality.

KINDS OF WASHI

Although there are dozens of types of washi, this section describes the general categories of washi that you are likely to find today. Traditionally, washi was formed and treated in special ways to produce paper for different purposes, therefore with different qualities. *Maniai-shi* included paper with clay added to keep it from puckering, especially useful when the paper will be hung from the wall as backing for artwork or a sign. Waterproof papers made by oiling washi with rapeseed were used for packaging, umbrellas, and raincoats. Tougher, thicker papers were made for tags and cards, while thinner papers, called *usuyo-shi*, were primarily used for filtration, packaging delicate items, and artful wrapping.

There are excellent books on washi that break these major categories into several subsets of washi types. Though the names of the same papers in different locations and countries have changed over time, resulting in some confusion, this book uses the most recent and common trade names, which you are likely to find in catalogs, on the Internet, and in paper shops. In this book we will focus on the techniques that will help you use washi successfully, regardless of its common name or makeup. The following descriptions and photos will help you to identify and select the proper washi for each project and give you an idea about the types of washi-like papers you may wish to make yourself.

natural washi

dyed washi

Natural washi is white to tan in color and is made from one or more of the three traditional washi fiber sources: Gampi (*Wikstroemia diplomorpha*), Mitsumata (*Edgeworthia chrysantha*), and Kozo (*Broussonetia papyrifera*). Natural washi may be brightened by drying in the sunlight, but it is usually not colored by additives such as dyes, pigments, or clay.

Dyed washi is available in many colors and weights. Dyes, however, are usually not light-fast, so be careful before you choose solid-colored washi for a project you want to display in sunlight or keep for generations.

chirigami

chiyogami

tie-dyed washi

momigami

Chirigami is natural washi with chopped bits of the dark bark included. The result is a rustic-looking paper, flecked with dark flakes and strands.

Chiyogami washi is decorated with patterns, animals, flowers, symbols, and auspicious icons, to illustrate traditional celebrations and the changing seasons. It is traditionally printed using woodblock techniques. Chiyogami stenciled with kimono fabric–inspired patterns, called yuzen, is also popular. Traditionally, a separate stencil or woodblock is used for each color.

Tie-dyed and/or **fold-dyed** washi is colorful, often with kaleidoscopic patterns that are produced by folding, twisting, tying, and dying the paper. Elaborate patterns result when the process is repeated using different dyes and other physical restraints, masks, or resists.

Momigami is washi that has been crumpled by hand to give the paper texture. A special paste, made from *konnyaku* starch from the root of the *Amorphophallus konjac*

unryu washi

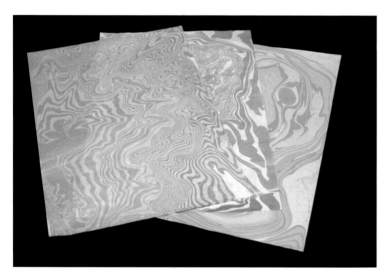

suminagashi

plant, is then applied, usually to one side only. The paper is then crumpled, opened, and crumpled again. Done repeatedly, the process develops an intricate surface texture, similar to crepe paper, and the sheet shrinks in size.

Unryu washi, also known as *unryushi*, has large pieces of partially beaten fibers included for texture, which create a floating cloud-like effect. Sometimes, patterned screens are raised through the vat of fibers and then applied to plain sheets of washi; these elements often resemble a "fiber-optic" effect, catching light in beautiful patterns of shimmering silkiness.

Suminagashi, meaning flowing ink, is marbled washi made by floating colored swirls of inks on water. As the washi is carefully laid on the ink swirls, the color is taken up into the washi, which is then dried. These delicate pastel patterns form pleasing, serendipitous designs.

USES FOR WASHI

Washi can be used for nearly everything, but, before you begin a project, consider the following historical perspective.

Ceremonial Use and Formal Documents

Probably the oldest use for washi is for special ceremonial use and for formal documents. Even today, the paper used for treaties, certificates, and important awards is often made with special fibers and careful processes, because it is expected to last for many generations.

Writing and Calligraphy

Writing and calligraphy are arts that demand papers of the finest qualities for permanence and elegance. In particular, *shodo*, Japanese brush calligraphy, requires specific qualities of paper to properly handle the style of inks used. The washi chosen should give the calligraphy life, working in concert with it, rather than becoming subjected by the forms of the calligraphic characters. There must be balance, and strong calligraphy requires more "white space" to give it room to breathe. With washi, that "white space" becomes an integral element of the piece, and not just emptiness.

Shoji Screens

The *shoji* screen is much more than a room partition or divider. For the Japanese, it organizes life itself into pleasant, illuminated, harmonious spaces. These versatile paper walls were originally erected as stand-alone structures, but later they were made to easily slide open or closed, quickly and efficiently converting space as more or less was needed. Shadows and sounds play on the screen's panels to enhance the mood of the space. Washi used for shoji screens is particularly clean and strong. After several months to a year, it is repaired or replaced, much as westerners spruce up their rooms with a new coat of paint. Simply hanging beautiful pieces of washi in windows with less than picturesque views is something that all of us can do to enjoy its qualities in the daylight.

Containers and Wrappings

The act of giving has been raised to an art form in Japan, similar to the elaborate process of the Japanese tea ceremony, with important symbolism associated with every element. It is common even for small items to be packaged with at least two, and often several, levels of containment, enhancing both the experience of receiving, as well as that of giving. This is why washi is commonly used to cover or make containers. The pleasing, often bright colors and patterns generate remarks of appreciation, leading to prolonged conversation during this important, gift-giving process. Often, the pattern or style of the paper container will contain a clue as to the contents. Usually it is simply beautiful, and somehow appropriate to the occasion or to the recipient. Washi containers such as boxes and vases are often used over and over again.

Impatient children today often tear through gift wrap before seeing anything except the size of the package, but in Japan, it is customary to politely savor the attractiveness of each level of wrapping around even the most humble of gifts or treats. Indeed, we have saved most of the washi wrappings and containers from the gifts we have received. These papers find new reincarnations as thank-you notes, folded ornaments, greeting cards, or cherished components of entries in our travel scrapbooks. Passing these beautiful papers on provides a simple way to establish a continuity for the relationship through the years.

Books

People love one-of-a-kind, handmade books, which seem to go through cycles of fashion. Books featuring unique, handmade papers are especially popular now. Many of our customers come looking for archival and decorative papers to complement their latest book-binding project. This has been one of the more popular projects using paper, because it is not difficult or expensive, and customized or personalized books always make great gifts.

Maybe you have found the perfect washi for a gift scrapbook. Maybe you want to print your own great novel, then lovingly bind it in handmade paper for casual display on your own (or perhaps your mother's) coffee table. Here is an opportunity for you to self-publish an heirloom!

Works of Art

Many of the customers who purchase our handmade papers are artists who appreciate painting, contact printing, or incorporating handmade papers into multimedia art. Abstract artists compose overlapping fields and shapes of different types of washi into collages of handmade paper. The art of composing torn bits of washi is a time-honored art called *chigiri-e*, or "torn paper pictures." In this art, different colors and textures of torn washi create collages of still life and scenery, similar to watercolors, yet composed entirely of handmade papers with no applied paints or inks. In *sumi-e*, Japanese ink painting, the strength of the brushstrokes, the line and form of the drawing, and the subtle gestures are enhanced by the way the specially-designed washi paper's fibers handle ink. Many types of washi take watercolors beautifully.

Lanterns

Famous artists and origami experts have made careers of illuminating washi. The warmth of the fiber sheets, the irregular clumps, knots, and deckle edges capture light in magical ways. Washi is naturally light and airy. When illuminated globes or other forms are suspended, they may evoke the moon and stars. With proper safeguarding, a washi lantern may be the best way to appreciate the various forms and types of handmade paper.

Be careful! Avoid using heat-producing bulbs or flames. Even if you know the watt limit of the fixture, the person replacing a light bulb could mistakenly use a high temperature halogen bulb. Newer LED (light-emitting diode) lighting could be a better choice, but we avoid this fire danger by never using electric lights or candles. We direct a spotlight onto the washi object from a safe distance, rather than risk a fire.

Kites

Washi is strong, so let the wind carry your spirits aloft on a washi kite. The paper kite was enjoyed in China before coming to Japan around 800 A.D. What better way to share a beautiful composition with the rest of the world? A kite above the horizon puts the world into perspective, for on the other end is a child at heart. Today, many kites are made of plastic film, but washi is quite strong enough to withstand winds. A washi kite also makes an excellent room decoration when it is not being flown. Your visitors will be able to appreciate its beauty up close, as well as far away.

Toys

Washi makes great toys! Folded or constructed toys, such as spinning tops, flapping birds, streamers, pinwheels, balloons, paper animals, and, of course, paper airplanes become treasured keepsakes when they are made of washi. Mobiles of paper animals or planes provide plenty of colors, shapes, and shadows to ponder. This book's techniques for covering objects will give you ideas about refreshing worn or tattered toys with beautiful washi, transforming them into cherished keepsakes as the child grows. While it is true that many washi toys are folded (origami), be careful not to consider using so-called "origami paper." Regular "origami paper" was developed for kindergarten use. Designed to allow children to explore folded forms and patterns, it was manufactured to be inexpensive and disposable. When we explain to students that we never use such origami paper for fine origami art, they seem surprised. When we show them two masterworks, one folded from inexpensive, wood pulp origami paper, and the other from washi, they instantly see that there is no comparison. The sculpture made from inexpensive, wood pulp paper with fugitive colorants becomes brittle and its colors fade. The masterwork folded from high-quality washi, colored using inorganic, ground mineral pigments, still looks as fresh as the day it was made, even though both pieces are the same age. Art folded from fine, handmade paper will be a cherished heirloom, while works folded from inexpensive papers will probably live on only as a memory or a photograph.

Decorative

There are so many colors, designs, patterns, and prints of washi that much of the fun is finding just the right piece to complement a room or table setting. Washi transforms the utilitarian pencil cup into a personal statement. It softens hard edges, brightens dull or boring plastic, and gives previously ugly things a chance to shine. Today's interior design professionals know that washi adds that special flair of fun or elegance to the décor or design. If you love washi, you will want it all around you.

MAKING WASHI

Making your own handmade paper is not an expensive or an unreasonable idea. Remember that paper has been made by hand for over 2,100 years by people with fewer resources than you. Making washi is "low tech," with simple tools and materials. There are many ways that you can try your hand at making several kinds of washi right at home. Though hard work, diligence, and lots of practice are the main ingredients in quality hand papermaking, you will see that today, several of the stages of making washi have been made much easier for the artist or hobbyist. Ready-to-use fibers, pigments, and equipment are available from specialty supply sources. With some care, even a novice can make perfectly usable, beautiful papers by hand at home.

We will present only the most basic steps in making washi. The following methods for preparing pulp and forming sheets will provide enough information for you not only to try it but to make paper for many of the projects in this book. These methods will also help you better understand, evaluate, and respect the washi you encounter in your travels.

PREPARING THE PULP

Demonstrated by Michael G. LaFosse

Kozo (*Broussonetia papyrifera*) paper mulberry, growing in our backyard.

This section demonstrates the most basic techniques for preparing pulp prior to making fine paper by hand. Traditional washi is most often formed from Kozo pulp. Compared to Mitsumata and Gampi, Kozo has the longest fibers, and it is easily cultivated. The materials you will need are readily available from the resources listed in this book (see page 127), and you may find other sources near you or listed on the Internet.

Materials

- Bast fiber from Kozo, Mitsumata, or Gampi, 1 pound (454 grams) of dry weight

- Alkali or "soda ash" (also known as "sodium carbonate"), 3.25 ounces (90 grams)

- Water, 2.5 gallons (9.5 liters)

- Formation aid (polyethylene oxide powder), 1 tablespoon (8 grams)

Equipment

- Scale

- Large stainless steel stockpot, 16–20 quart (15–19 liter)

- Stove

- Large, stainless steel stirring spoon

- Deep vat, 36″ x 24″ x 8″ (91cm x 61cm x 20cm), for sheet forming (inexpensive polyethylene vats are commonly sold in home improvement stores for mixing mortar)

- Long vinyl or rubber gloves

- Splash goggles, dust mask, and apron

- Cotton cloth

- Fine stainless steel strainer sieve

- Wooden mallets for beating

- Clear glass jar for jar test

- Blender

- Pitcher or bowl

- Mechanical pulp beater (optional)

Above left: A sample of different types of screens, deckles, and frames used in hand papermaking; Right: Alkali (soda ash, or sodium carbonate) with dried, Kozo bast fibers from the paper mulberry.

1 Weigh 1 pound (454 grams) of dry fiber and soak in plenty of water overnight. Bast fibers swell after being wetted.

2 Measure enough alkali: 20 percent of the dry weight of the batch of fiber to be cooked, so use 3.25 ounces (92 grams) of alkali, per pound (454 grams) of dry fiber. (Wear vinyl gloves, a dust mask, and an apron. Work in a well-ventilated area.) Bring 2.5 gallons (9.5 liters) of water to a near boil. Carefully add the alkali to the hot water. Stir to dissolve.

3 Carefully add the soaked bast fibers. Bring to a gentle boil and then lower the heat to maintain a simmer. Stir every half hour. Normally, batches take approximately four hours of simmering.

4 Place a damp cloth (an old pillowcase or a double layer of cheesecloth works well) in a stainless steel mesh strainer basket. Thoroughly rinse the cooked bast fibers under the faucet. If desired, remove any last bits of impurities, including any bark, knots, and undigested clumps that could contaminate the paper. (You can leave these impurities in if you wish to make "chirigami," which has its own appeal.)

5 Wring the rinsed fiber by making baseball-sized wads for beating. This ball is ready for beating.

6 Manually beating the wet fiber with a wooden paddle or mallet splays and separates the strands of fiber and also hydrates the cellulose. The goal is not to shorten the fibers but to add exposed surface area, which will result in finer, stronger sheets. Regular but gentle pounding will allow more water into the fibers and make them swell. It will take about ten to fifteen minutes per ball to properly process the fiber. Stop beating every minute or so to add a little water. Each ball may require up to ¼ cup (59 milliliters) of water to be added during the beating stage. This "water of hydration" activates potential bonding sites on the cellulose strands, so stronger paper requires more water during beating.

7 Use the "jar test" to measure your progress by dropping a small sample of beaten pulp into a beaker of water.

8 Stir briskly for a few moments until the fibers are well separated. When the fibers have reached the stage of being properly beaten, there will be no clumps in the suspension.

Should you decide to skip the above steps, pre-processed pulp is available. The fiber is ready for hydrating. (The fiber shown here is abaca, from the *Musa textilus* plant, and is available by the pound, obtained as thick sheets from papermaking supply companies. The bag contains "formation aid," polyethylene oxide powder.) We recommend using pre-processed abaca rather than "traditional" washi fibers such as Kozo for your first experiments in Japanese-style papermaking, so you can avoid the laborious and messy alkaline cooking process. Doing so will allow you to focus on getting the knack of sheet forming, while eliminating many of the variables that could complicate your efforts.

Soak the pre-processed sheets of pulp in plenty of water and agitate to sufficiently separate the fibers. Use the jar test to see when your pulp is ready for sheet forming.

If you have access to a mechanical beater, such as this one built by Valley Iron Works originally for laboratory use by a paper mill, you can more precisely control the variables of beating time and pressure against the bedplate. More and more schools and universities offer papermaking courses. You may find that a nearby school has a studio with a paper pulp beater that you can use.

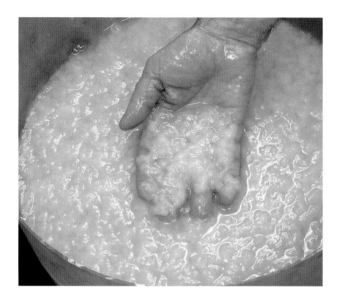

9 This pulp is ready for sheet forming. It feels soft and plump with water. You can rinse the stockpot well and use that to hold the pulp.

10 Prepare a solution of formation aid by filling a blender to the halfway mark with water. While the motor is running on low speed, gradually add (sprinkle) up to one tablespoon (½ fluid ounce, or 15 cc) of the polyethylene oxide powder. Listen carefully to the sound of the motor, and stop adding when the motor begins to labor.

Formation aid makes the water in the sheet-forming vat more viscous and slippery. This prevents the long fibers from tangling and knotting, allowing for the formation of a thin, even sheet. Formation aid also slows down the drainage of water, allowing plenty of time for the papermaker to control the flow of slurry across the surface of the mold.

11 Pour the formation aid solution into a pitcher or bowl, cover, and let it stand overnight. It is important to let the formation aid stand to allow all of the particles to completely dissolve and for any bubbles to clear. Blended formation aid is quite viscous and slippery. Clean up floor spills immediately to prevent accidents.

Traditional Japanese recipes use vegetable mucilage, called *neri*, derived from the root of the *tororo-aoi* plant (and others), which is mashed, soaked, and strained before use.

12 Charge a vat of water with enough beaten pulp to make it cloudy with dispersed fiber.

This papermaking session began with 1½ pounds (680 grams, dry weight of fiber) of pulp. We added half the pulp to the vat, which contained 50 gallons (190 liters) of water. Forming each sheet of paper removes a small amount of pulp from the vat, so it is necessary to regularly add measured portions of pulp, to maintain a fairly consistent concentration of fiber in the vat. We typically add about a pint (0.5 liter) of pulp to the vat after every fourth sheet. This is only a guide; you should experiment or measure what works best for you.

13 Viscous formation aid is added to the vat containing the pulp. This will cause the water to become viscous and make a "blurpy," bubbly sound when stirred. Do not make the water too viscous or drainage will be too slow and fibers will not deposit evenly on the screen. Form a test sheet to see how quickly the screen drains. Gradually add more formation aid until the draining time increases enough to give you good control of the slurry flow across the screen. It is easier to add more formation aid if the screen drains too quickly. You can speed the draining to some degree by agitating the vat, breaking down some of the viscosity.

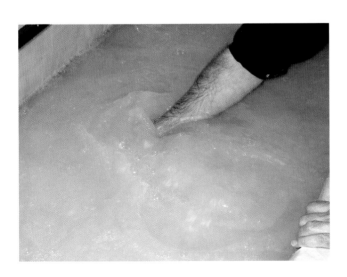

14 To keep the pulp in suspension, gently agitate the water as necessary before you begin to form a new sheet of paper. Mixing the pulp by hand disperses it evenly within the vat of water.

TAME-ZUKI: "RETAINING METHOD" OF PAPERMAKING

(also known as "Western-Style")

Demonstrated by Michael G. LaFosse

Tame-zuki means making paper (*suku*) by accumulation, containment (*tameru*), or retention of the watery pulp. This name refers to the frame, or deckle, which is placed over the screen, which corrals and contains a quantity of the pulp slurry while the water drains through the screen. Unlike Nagashizuki (see page 32), slurry is not thrown off. The papermaker must regularly adjust the amount of fiber in the vat to create sheets of uniform thickness. Add more pulp to the vat for thicker sheets and less pulp for thinner sheets.

Materials

■ Prepared pulp (Kozo, Mitsumata, or Gampi), 1 pound (454 grams) dry weight

■ Plenty of water

■ Formation aid (polyethylene oxide solution) (optional. See Preparing the Pulp on page 20)

Equipment

■ Deep vat, 36″ x 24″ x 8″ (91cm x 61cm x 20cm), for sheet forming (inexpensive polyethylene vats are commonly sold in home improvement stores for mixing mortar)

■ Papermaker's mold and deckle, 11″ x 17″ (28cm x 43cm) or smaller

■ Two dozen or more felt rectangles (synthetic polyester "chamois" or natural wool), cut 2″ (5cm) larger than the mold, soaked in water

■ Four rectangles of plywood, ½″ (1cm) thick, cut to the same size as the wool felts

■ 20-ton hydraulic bottle jack

■ Press frame

■ Miscellaneous blocks for safe pressing

■ Paper blotters, cut to the same size as the felts

■ Corrugated cardboard, cut to the same size as the felts

■ Box fan, 20″ x 20″ (51cm x 51cm)

■ Plastic sheeting (or garbage can liners) and duct tape to direct air from the box fan through the post of blotters and pressed pulp

■ Ratchet straps (or duct tape) to secure the enclosure around the post in the drying box

1 Here is a western-style screen with removable deckle (frame). The frame's thickness acts as a dam to retain *(tame-zuki)* a specific quantity of the pulp slurry.

2 The deckle is fitted onto the flat side of the screen and held firmly together.

3 The mold is plunged into the vat of prepared pulp, bottom edge first, and pulled forward and under the surface of the slurry.

4 The screen and deckle are raised while leveling off.

5 The water drains through the pulp and screen.

6 The wet pulp shines on the surface of the screen.

7 After removing the deckle frame, notice the "deckle edge," or rough edge, along the rectangular sheet of wet pulp.

8 The edge of the screen is aligned to the side of the wet orange felts in the black tub.

9 The screen is inverted and the wet pulp is transferred onto the wet felts with pressure applied to the underside of the screen. The wet felts are compressible, and, as the screen is pushed onto the felt, the paper pulp is pulled off the screen by the suction created as pressure is released.

10 One end of the screen is raised, showing the pulp sheet left behind on the wet felt. The wet pulp is quite translucent.

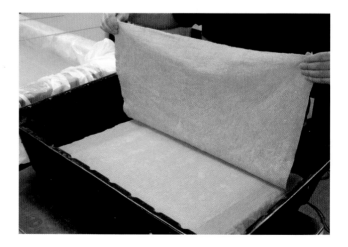

11 Another wet felt is laid gently over the wet pulp, thus building a stack (called a "post") of alternating felts and pulp layers. As pulp is removed from the vat, more is added. About a pint (0.5 liters) of beaten pulp produces about two sheets of 16 inch by 20 inch (41cm by 51cm) paper, so a pint of slurry is added to the vat after every two to four dips, depending on the desired thickness of the sheet.

PRESSING THE FORMED SHEETS

Why press the paper? It removes much of the water, thus reducing drying time and drying energy. It also allows the papermaker to impart a uniform finish on each side of the paper. There are many ways to press newly formed sheets of paper. One could purchase a papermaker's press for several thousands of dollars, but remember that the earliest papermaking methods did not involve pressing the paper at all: Screens were simply left in the sunlight to dry until the matted fibers could be peeled off in a single sheet. In the past, I pressed my handmade paper by laying the stack of alternating felts and couched pulp sandwiched between plywood boards, then parking the front wheel of my car squarely on the center of the top board.

When we make large sheets of paper at Origamido Studio, we couch the wet pulp onto a large piece of felt stretched over a smooth table, cover it with plastic sheeting, and then insert a suction hose from a vacuum pump to enable atmospheric pressure to press the paper. Richard has also set up various contraptions to press my handmade paper. One involved a 12-foot lumber lever weighted with a steel drum that he filled with water from a garden hose. The most successful involved a 20-ton capacity hydraulic bottle jack, available for well under $100. With this jack, we have taken our papermaking classes "on the road," and so we built a simple, versatile pressing frame from lightweight aluminum struts and threaded rods. Only 2½ inches (6cm) thick, it hangs on the wall (just like a picture frame) when not in use.

How much pressure do you need? We make great paper that measures 16 inches by 20 inches (or 320 square inches), and, with a 20-ton (40,000 pound capacity) jack, it must be pressed at less than 125 pounds per square inch. Because the boards we use to press the felts are 20 inches by 28 inches (560 square inches), the actual pressure on the paper is probably less than 70 pounds per square inch. This amount of pressure removes enough water for our paper to be bone dry in the morning after staying in the fan box overnight.

Note: It is great to be inventive, but please pay attention to safety, especially when blocking or jacking great forces. Cars roll. Jacks kick out. Wood blocks under pressure can split and fail. Never place anyone, including any part of your own body, in a danger zone. Have an engineer review what you are trying to do to prevent something dangerous. Center, check, and double check the placement of the blocks and jacks. Use redundant safety devices, such as double ties, double nuts, and double-thick boards. Stow boards and blocks where they can't fall. Keep children and spectators away, just in case.

12 Origamido Studio co-founder and papermaker Richard L. Alexander presses the paper to remove excess water and make the sheets thinner. He is using a 20-ton capacity, hydraulic bottle jack to apply force to the post of alternating layers of felt and pulp, sandwiched between pieces of marine plywood and other lumber, within a portable press frame. There are four ¾ inch by 36 inches (2cm by 91cm) vertical threaded rods holding the horizontal, wood-filled, square struts of aluminum. (The photo shows an end view. The other three rods are hidden.)

13 As pressure is applied, water from the felts drains back into the vat.

14 After the post is removed from the press, I peel a sheet of pressed, wet paper pulp off the felt.

15 The newly formed sheet of wet paper pulp is laid on top of a thick, absorbent paper blotter (cut slightly longer and slightly wider than the wet paper). The blotter material must be able to wick moisture from the wet pulp while retaining physical form. One would not use paper towels because the fibers are too loose. Similarly, one would not use cloth towels because the weave would integrate with the pulp fibers, making it difficult to separate when dry.

16 A piece of corrugated cardboard separates each sandwich of blotter/wet paper/blotter. All of the openings in the corrugation run in the same direction.

17 This is a view of a typical batch of paper made at Origamido Studio, looking through the post of stacked blotters, wet paper, and corrugated cardboard.

18 A 20-inch (51cm) box fan is built into the removable front panel of the two-piece, corrugated-plastic drying box. The front panel is held against the sides and top with two adjustable belts (ratchet straps). Notice that the top of the drying box is weighted with boards previously used to press the post, and, as the paper dries, the sides can move independently of the face panel containing the fan. A batch such as this, with seventy to one hundred sheets, dries completely overnight.

(Corrugated polyethylene plastic, used here, has become a favorite fabrication material for designers of signs, returnable boxes, recycling containers, and even U.S. Post Office letter bins. Many packaging supply companies carry it in several colors. We also dry paper by directing air from the fan through the post with plastic sheeting and duct tape.)

19 A finished sheet of paper is separated from the blotter.

NAGASHIZUKI: SHEET-FORMING TECHNIQUE

Demonstrated by Michael G. LaFosse

In contrast to the retaining method, the equipment used in this technique forces the papermaker to choose how much slurry will pass through the screen. The remainder is "thrown off" in an artful and beautiful, but tricky, technique. With a little practice, a beginner can make acceptable paper, but it can take years to learn the proper timing to eject exactly the right amount of pooled slurry to produce paper with a clean edge.

Materials

- Prepared pulp (Kozo, Mitsumata, or Gampi), 1 pound (454 grams) of dry weight

- Plenty of water

- Formation aid (polyethylene oxide solution) (See Preparing the Pulp on page 20)

- Spool of lightweight string or thread, to be cut into pieces, one for each sheet, approximately 2″ (5 cm) longer than the long edge of the sheets being formed

Equipment

- Deep vat, 36″ x 24″ x 8″ (91cm x 61cm x 20cm), for sheet forming (inexpensive polyethylene vats are commonly sold in home improvement stores for mixing mortar)

- Japanese-style papermaker's frame and screen (*sugeta*), 33″ x 21″ (84cm x 53cm) or smaller

- Two rectangles of marine varnished plywood, ½″ (1cm) thick, cut 2″ (5cm) larger than the sheets to be made

- Two pieces of felt cut the same size as the plywood boards

- Soft-bristle, wide wallpaper brush

- Drying board or glass, mounted securely in a vertical position, at least 5″ (13cm) larger than the sheets to be made. Note: A bamboo *su* is not necessary. A western-style mold can be substituted if a deep deckle (at least ¾″ [2cm] deep) is used with the Tame-zuki method of couching and drying the paper (see steps 6 through 19).

1 This is a bamboo *su* (papermaking screen) being soaked in water prior to forming sheets. We allow it to soak for several hours, often overnight.

2 The *su* is placed on the hinged frame; the set is often called a *sugeta*.

3 An imminent plunge!

4 The scoop: The bottom edge enters first. The back is lowered while the front is raised and pulled forward to catch a charge of the pulp slurry.

5 The first charge of pulp slurry floods the screen, forming the first "skin" as the water drains through. The slurry travels forward.

6 The screen is charged again, and the fresh slurry is rocked back to front repeatedly. This action deposits a new layer of pulp over the first skin. The water will drain more slowly at this stage.

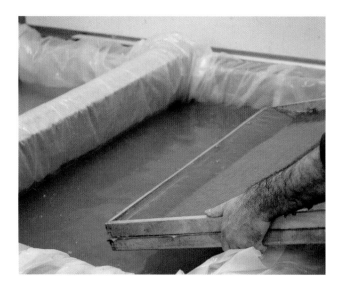

7 The far end of the mold is tipped down to collect remaining slurry before it is tossed back into the vat.

8 The excess slurry is tossed back into the vat.

9 The screen is charged again, and the new slurry is rocked side to side repeatedly, to build a cross-grain arrangement of fibers in the sheet. Unlike the retaining method, which depends on a random arrangement of the

fibers as the slurry drains, this method allows the paper-maker to impart any degree of grain (or general orientation of the fibers).

10 The far end of the mold is tipped down again to collect remaining slurry before it is tossed back into the vat. The slurry is tossed to the back of the vat.

This technique helps to make a cleaner, more uniform edge.

11 Once the desired number of layers has been built up, the sheet is ready to be removed from the mold as the hinged frame is opened.

12 The bamboo su is removed.

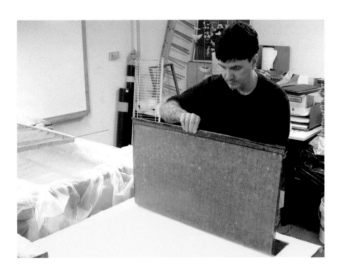

13 The pulp is being laid against a wet, yellow felt.

14 The front of the su is firmly pressed down to make sure the edge of wet pulp stays behind as the su is raised.

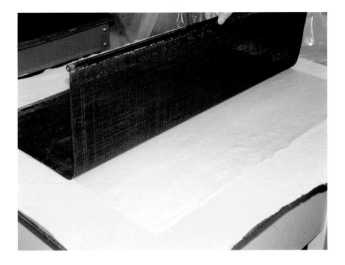

15 The wet pulp remains on the wet felt, as the su is raised and removed.

16 Before subsequent sheets of wet pulp are couched on top of the first, a piece of string is laid across the front to aid separation. Unlike the Tame-zuki method (see page 26), no separating layers of felt are needed.

17 The blotted and pressed sheets are easily separated from each other. If just a few sheets are to be formed, pressing is not needed, because small batches may be blotted with other felts.

18 The wet sheet is lifted away by its adjacent corners. The wide brush will be used to apply the wet sheet to the drying surface.

19 The right top corner of the sheet is applied first to the drying surface. The sheet is brushed diagonally from upper right to lower left. This Formica tabletop works great for drying large sheets of paper. (We dry paper against sheets of glass when we desire paper with a shiny surface.)

20 The sheet is brushed downward from the diagonal to secure the lower half, and then brushed upward from the diagonal to secure the upper half.

21 The process is completed by brushing along the top. The sheet is allowed to dry. The paper will sometimes separate as it dries, aiding removal.

ADDING EMBEDDED OBJECTS:
HANDMADE PAPER WITH FLOWER INCLUSIONS

Demonstrated by Richard L. Alexander

Whenever you get the chance to make paper by hand, it is fun to include other objects, perhaps some of the flower blossoms or plants that might be in season. This is a kind of "date stamp" that you will fondly recall later on. Flowers, leaves, or petals incorporate nicely into the washi, which can become greeting cards, place cards, or window hangings, acting as "light catchers" when sunlight shines through the flowers to bring their spirit to life again. Make sure that the inclusions are fairly flat and that their colors will not bleed more than you want them to. You can use either Tame-zuki or Nagashizuki methods for sheet forming.

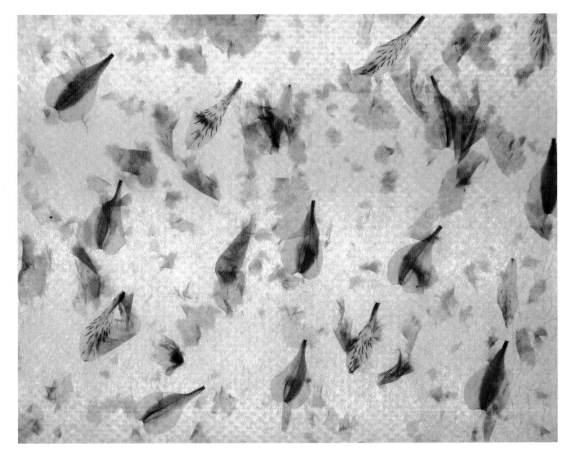

A finished piece, "Falling Petals," with backlighting, by Richard L. Alexander.

1 Couch one layer of paper pulp onto a wet felt. Arrange fresh or dried leaves and flower petals in a pleasing manner.

2 Couch a second, thin layer of paper pulp onto the arrangement, forming a composite of paper pulp/plant inclusions/paper pulp between the wet felts.

3 This is the resulting panel, after the paper is pressed and dried.

4 Here is another arrangement.

5 After pressing to flatten and remove excess water, remove the sheet from the felt before drying.

Here is a close-up view after pressing.

This finished piece has been used as a display surface for origami butterflies.

A pressed plant, with backlighting, by Richard L. Alexander.

A finished piece, "Fanciful Plant," with backlighting, by Richard L. Alexander.

FOLDED TIE-DYED WASHI

Traditional coloring method demonstrated by Michael G. LaFosse

Materials

- Washi

- Permanent liquid inks or dyes of various colors

Equipment

- Shallow metal pans or dishes for dye

- Plastic sheeting (polyethylene drop cloth)

- Knife or scissors to cut the ends off the folded washi

- Rubber or vinyl gloves

Tie-dyed washi is colorful, often with kaleidoscopic patterns that are produced by folding, twisting, tying, and dyeing the paper. The folded tie-dyed method is simple to do and gives one-of-a-kind patterns to washi you have made yourself, or it may be used to personalize washi that you have purchased. Geometric, yet organic, these elaborate patterns result when the process is repeated using different dyes, ties, and other masks or resists between stages.

1 Use a rectangle of plain, white washi.

2 Begin the process of fan-folding by first folding the rectangle in half.

3 Bring the edge that is closest to you across to meet the far edge; crease in the middle (making fourths).

4 Bring the new edge that is closest to you across to meet the far edge; crease in the middle (making eighths).

5 Open.

6 Re-crease some of the panels so the folds alternate between mountains and valleys (fan-fold). Gather the panels and make sure their edges align.

7 Fold up one corner at the end to meet the imaginary mid-line. Press down firmly on the resulting mountain fold that stops at the corner. This sets up a 60-degree angle.

8 Fold the end back and forth, alternating diagonally, so that the strip of panels becomes a triangular stack of layers.

9 Now the pre-creasing is complete.

10 Experiment with basic shapes and variations; for instance, using a sharp knife, carefully cut the ends off the three points of the triangular stack for a laced effect.

11 Here we fan-fold a long strip to create stacked squares, rather than triangles.

12 Here is the finished stack of squares, ready for dyeing.

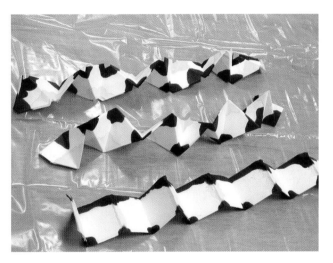

13 Dip each corner into different colors of ink or dye. The longer you hold an edge into the dye, the farther the ink will migrate from the edge.

14 Allow the washi to dry on a plastic drop cloth, before unfolding.

15 Open the folded sheet carefully to reveal your patterns.

BACK-COATING

Demonstrated by Michael G. LaFosse

ack-coating is an essential technique for preparing washi for a variety of uses. It allows you to select different types (color, pattern, or weight) of papers for the front and the back of your project; it allows you to stiffen the material to produce sufficient body for working a three-dimensional project; and it allows you to impart qualities into the composite that are not present when using either sheet alone. For example, washi that would not be good for folding becomes superb when back-coated with another sheet of an appropriate type of paper.

1 Trim one of the sheets to be approximately ½ inch (1cm) shorter on all sides. Lightly mist the papers on both sides. Allow a few moments for the moisture to become fully absorbed into the paper.

Incorporating water into the paper allows the paper to expand. Adding water to the paper causes it to expand locally. This prevents the paper from puckering when paste is applied, because paste contains water. Without adding water, the dry paper pulls water out of the paste, which would cause the paste to thicken and become difficult to spread.

Materials

- Two sheets of paper (washi and backing)
- Starch-based glue or paste
- Small scrap of paper

Equipment

- Spray bottle of water
- Drying board (foamcore, plywood, glass, or other stiff material larger than the largest of your chosen papers)
- Glue brush (China Bristle), 3″ (8cm) wide to apply the paste
- Dish for glue
- Wide brush
- Knife

2 Lay the display side of the larger sheet of washi down against the surface of the table. Brush paste evenly on the exposed underside.

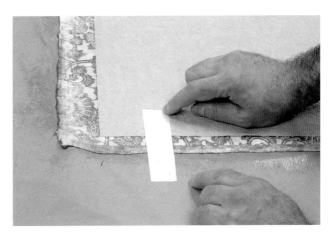

3 Lay the back of the smaller sheet directly and squarely onto the pasted underside of the first sheet.

4 Use a scrap of paper as a "gateway" that will allow you to insert a knife easily between the board and the paper after the glue dries.

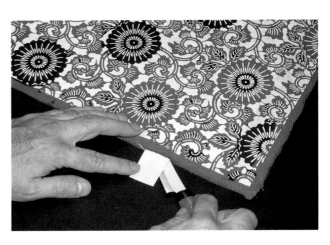

5 Carefully flip the back-coated assembly onto a smooth, hard drying surface, such as a piece of glass, plastic, or plywood. Use a wide brush to smooth the sheet. This applies the glued margin to the board's surface.

6 After the back-coated paper has dried, insert a knife through the gateway.

7 Carefully release the paper from the board by sliding the knife along the pasted margin.

8 Trim the edges before use.

PROJECTS

The projects in this book represent a wide cross-section of uses for washi, including a few traditional projects, as well as several contemporary, every-day, useful objects. These projects are suitable uses for the generally available types of Japanese washi, and the types of washi-like papers you can make yourself. Many arts and crafts stores, including some large chain stores, stock several types of washi. The Internet also allows up-to-the-minute sourcing for decorative and handmade papers, including Japanese washi.

Similarly, the other materials and equipment used for these projects are not exotic, nor hard-to-find, and each has common substitutes. One of the best aspects of working with washi is that it has been done for centuries; therefore, the equipment is usually low-tech, readily available, or easily made. For generations, these types of objects were made with love by hand, without sophisticated materials and methods.

As with any folk art, the vision you impart into the products of your hands is the mark you leave to the world. Out of respect for the washi, and the generations of craftspeople that created your beautiful washi, please take the time to read through this entire section to thoroughly understand the project. Be sure to measure and cut accurately, and practice whatever skill is required (folding, stitching, or back-coating) using less valuable paper until you have a sufficient grasp of the task to use the "good stuff."

As you proceed, please refer to the Symbols Key on page 128, which explains the diagrams used throughout this book.

HONORED TRADITIONS

Japanese Origami Crane

Ehiroi ▪ *Imoseyama* ▪ *Seigaiha*

Hana Tsutsumi ▪ *Noshi Awabi*

JAPANESE ORIGAMI CRANE

Introduction by Greg Mudarri

Traditional design demonstrated by Michael G. LaFosse

The crane, and the origami crane developed in Japan several hundred years ago, has long been a symbol of longevity. In Asian mythology, it is said that cranes live for 1,000 years. Cranes choose only one mate and never separate. Because of this, cranes have become an important symbol at wedding ceremonies.

The origami crane is the most widely recognized origami model around the world. If a person knows only one origami model, it is usually the crane, and so the Japanese origami crane now represents the totality of origami, and Japan itself. More recently, it has become a powerful international symbol of peace.

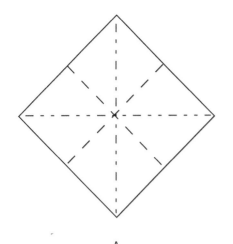

1 Fold in half four times as shown, creating mountain and valley folds as indicated: Begin with the square on the table with the color side up, fold diagonally to make a white triangle. Unfold, turn 90 degrees, repeat. Place the colored side down, and then fold the opposite sides of the square together. This is called a "book-fold." Open, rotate, and repeat to book-fold in the other direction, resulting in alternating mountains and valleys radiating from the center point. The white side of the paper in the photo shows this pre-crease pattern used to create what is often called the Preliminary Form.

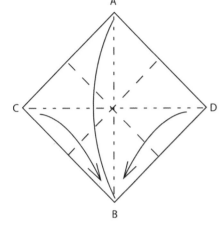

2 Collapse the form into a square, or diamond shape, using the existing creases. (In Diagram 2, Corners A, C, and D are collapsed to meet B.) Notice the arrangement of the layers.

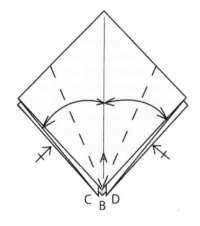

3 Pairs of cut edges are brought to the centerline of the diamond to form pre-creases for the upcoming "petal-fold," also called a "wing-fold." Repeat this on the back side, and then unfold.

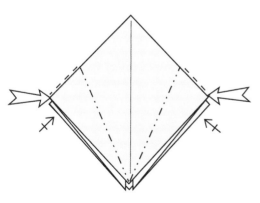

4 Push the indicated corners inward to "inside-reverse" both of the side corners on the diamond, tucking them beneath the upper layer of paper. Turn the model over and repeat.

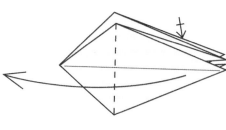

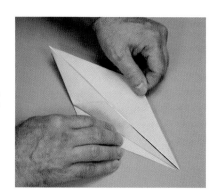

5 Your paper should look like this.

Fold the top layer by lifting the free corner up to form an elongated rhombus, or diamond shape. Repeat on the other side. Look ahead at step 6 for the result.

6 Your paper will look like this. Notice the split in the lower half of the diamond.

7 Fold in the lower edge pairs of the elongated diamond to the split. This will "skinny" the neck and tail. It is best to not allow these edges to touch. A hairline space will make the next step easier.
Repeat on the other side.

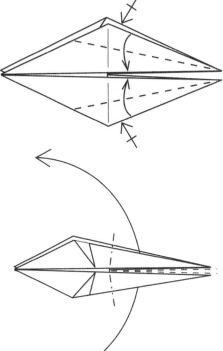

8 All four edges have been folded to the split, two on the front and two on the back. Inside-reverse fold the skinny corners upward. Look ahead at step 9 for the shape.

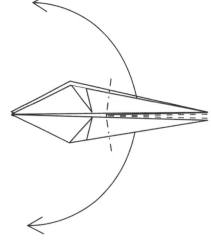

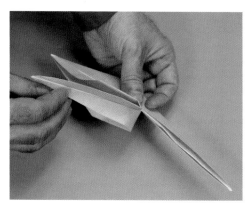

9 This photo (left) shows the inside-reverse fold in action: Pull the bottom point up, closing it between the two wings, as you set the desired angle.

10 Both points have been inside-reverse folded. Notice their symmetry, right.

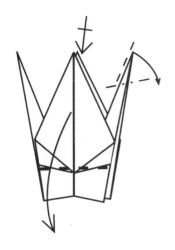

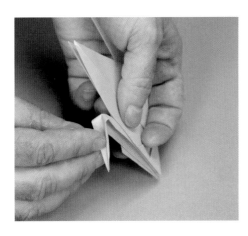

11 Inside-reverse fold the beak: Push the top point downward and inward, closing it between the two halves of the neck, as you set the desired angle of the beak. Fold the wings down.

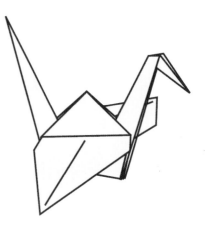

12 Notice that the wing has been folded down as far as possible. Repeat with the other wing.

13 Here is the finished Japanese Origami Crane with outstretched wings. (Pull the wings gently to create a fuller body.)

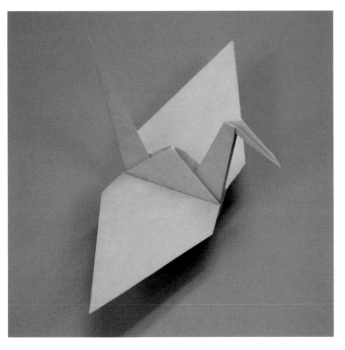

ORIGAMI PEACE CRANES

by Greg Mudarri

Left: Greg Mudarri making a peace offering of *senbazuru* ("one thousand cranes") on August 6, 2005, the sixtieth anniversary of the bombing of Hiroshima.

Right: The monument depicts Sadako Sasaki's spirit rising in hope above suffering.

The origami crane has become a symbol of world peace. Its popularity has grown partly because of books telling the sad story of Sadako Sasaki. She was only two years old when the atomic bomb was dropped on her home city of Hiroshima during World War II. Although seemingly unharmed, she developed leukemia nine years later. She strived to fold 1,000 cranes in accordance with the old Japanese legend that if one folds 1,000 cranes their wish will be granted. Although many accounts claim that she was unable to fold 1,000, she in fact managed to fold approximately 1,300 cranes. Sadly, she lost her life within a year of her diagnosis. Her story touched many people around the world and a new, remarkable peace movement began. Thousands of people make pilgrimages to memorial parks to deliver garlands of 1,000 cranes (called *senbazuru*) as a tangible expression of their wish for peace.

I visited the Peace Park in Hiroshima on August 6, 2005, the sixtieth anniversary of the bombing, and delivered my third garland of 1,000 cranes on that day. It was an emotional experience. More than 50,000 attended the ceremony. Many hundreds of people brought together millions upon millions of colored cranes, an expression that spoke louder than any words.

SENBAZURU: "THOUSAND CRANES"

Traditional design demonstrated by Greg Mudarri

Here are variations of *senbazuru*.

The Japanese word *senbazuru* indeed means "one thousand cranes," but the term is used for a style of connected cranes as well as for actual garlands of 1,000 cranes. In Japanese, the words representing "100" or "1,000" are often used to express "many," "unlimited variation," or "endless possibility," even when the subject is clearly countable. The oldest known published book on origami, *Hiden Senbazuru Orikata (The Secret of One Thousand Cranes)*, was published in 1797 and showed several ways of folding different versions and combinations of the crane. The long fibers of washi allow many to be folded from the same sheet while still connected at the corners (wingtips, beak, or tail). There surely are not 1,000 cranes in the book, but it does include one senbazuru design of one hundred connected cranes, created by folding one sheet of paper with many cuts. We have reintroduced some of those classic models here. Try folding them with different kinds of washi.

EHIROI

Traditional design demonstrated by Greg Mudarri

E hiroi is a depiction of *Oya Ko*, or "Parent and Child." The mother crane is feeding her young chick. The two are connected only at their beaks by a fine strand of washi.

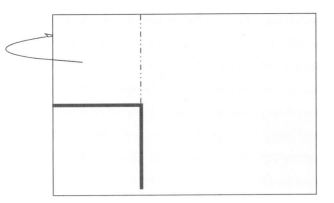

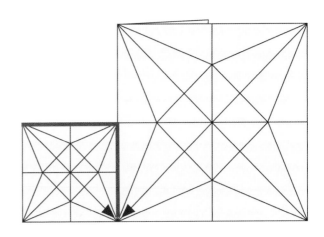

1 The paper is a 2 to 3 rectangle. The mother crane will be of the largest square size possible, leaving two squares on the side that are each one-fourth the size of the mother crane's square. Cut the paper as shown, making sure to leave the squares connected with just enough paper to ensure they will stay together. Folders typically hide the top square under the mother crane so that it disappears when the layers are folded together (but you may also trim it off).

2 The cranes will remain joined at their beaks.

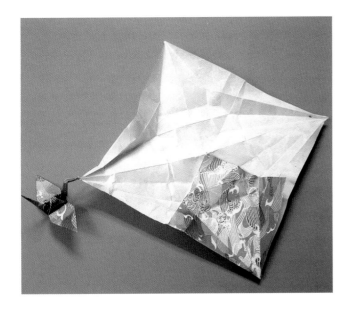

3 This is a view of the back side, showing the folded chick, and the top of the excess paper to be hidden by folding along with that corner of the larger square.

4 Here is the completed Ehiroi Mother Crane Feeding Young Chick.

IMOSEYAMA

Traditional design demonstrated by Greg Mudarri

I moseyama roughly translates to "sisters." This is a wonderful project to consider when the washi you have is beautiful on both sides, because they are equally displayed. These cranes are the same size, and they share a wing. Symbolizing togetherness, kindred spirits, or union, this composition makes a powerful statement and a treasured gift. Use a 2 to 1 rectangle of washi.

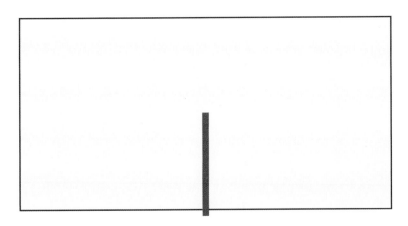

1 Cut the paper only halfway through the middle. This is so the cranes will share a wing.

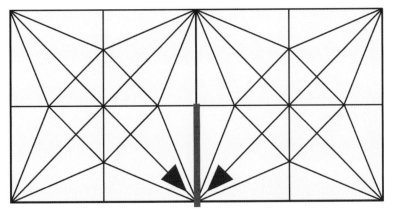

2 After cutting, fold the paper in half and fold one bird base while the squares are overlapped. Unfold enough to bring the two cranes apart, and reconstruct them using the existing folds. When complete, you will produce two cranes of different colors, joined at the wing.

Sister Cranes, shown beside a 2 to 1 rectangle, cut halfway through at the center. Notice the pre-creases after the folded paper is opened, ready to be re-folded to form the two cranes.

Here is the completed Imoseyama Sister Cranes, showing the shared wing.

SEIGAIHA

Traditional design demonstrated by Greg Mudarri

T ranslating to "Blue Ocean Wave," the *Seigaiha* senbazuru form creates an undulating and pleasing pattern, not only in its final form but also in its folding process. The experience of folding it can be quite therapeutic, similar to watching the waves roll in.

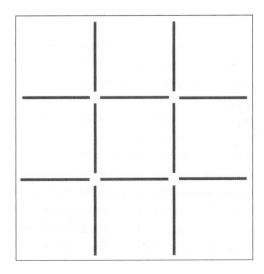

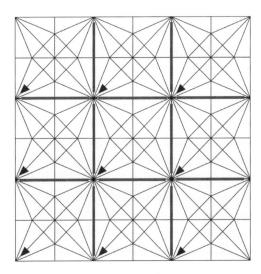

1 Fold a square paper into equal thirds, both horizontally and vertically, dividing the square into nine smaller squares. The slits will be cut in between each square as shown, but be sure never to cut through the critical corners.

2 Fold each third in half. Cutting through the newly folded edge makes it easier to perform this configuration of slits for the nine-crane Blue Ocean Wave.

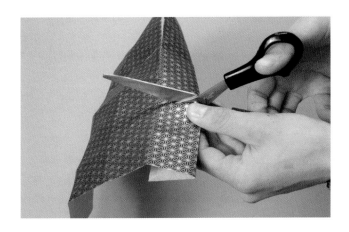

3 Fold nine cranes all facing the same direction to complete the Seigaiha.

4 It is easier to fold each step of each crane before proceeding to the next step in the folding process. This photo shows a semi-folded, nine-crane Blue Ocean Wave at the "bird base" stage.

5 Here is the completed Seigaiha, Blue Ocean Wave, with nine cranes.

NOSHI (TSUTSUMI)

by Greg Mudarri

Tsutsumi is the Japanese word for wrappers. *Noshi* are a particular kind of tsutsumi. The term *noshi* comes from the Japanese verb *nosu*, which means to stretch. The term noshi is used here not because the paper is stretched; rather, it is derived from the term *noshita awabi*, which translates to "stretched abalone." The term noshi, according to its original meaning, was only appropriate when applied to the tsutsumi used for stretched and dried abalone meat.

Abalone meat was considered a gift of good fortune in early Japan, so a special tsutsumi was used to present the gift, called *Noshi Awabi No Tsutsumi*. There is a Buddhist custom to refrain from eating meat at sad times, so the *Noshi Awabi* were given as a gift, or an attachment to a gift, to signify a joyous occasion when the abalone could be enjoyed.

Many different tsutsumi were used with gifts at special celebrations and were used as wrappings for flowers, fans, chopsticks, brushes, and sake bottles. They were often used as common attachments to gifts at important occasions, much like gift tags. From "noshita awabi" to "noshi awabi" and finally just "noshi," the meaning of the term for this specific kind of tsutsumi has changed a great deal. Now it is often used for all kinds of tsutsumi.

Why not try using these noshi for your own gifts or decorations? They are most often folded from a solid-color washi. White or natural paper was particularly favored in old Japan for noshi, as uncolored things were considered more honest, natural, and pure. Important Buddhist, Shinto, and other sacred rites often incorporate fine, white paper to symbolize purity, simplicity, and beauty.

HANA TSUTSUMI

Traditional design demonstrated by Greg Mudarri

*H*ana *Tsutsumi* means "flower wrapping." There are many noshi that are designated for giving specific types of flowers. This particular wrapping is suitable for either tree flowers or ground flowers.

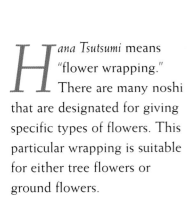

1 This shows the Hana Tsutsumi crease pattern. Using a square, first fold it in half to form a triangle.

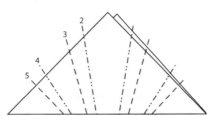

2 Pre-crease along the folds 2, 3, 4, and 5.

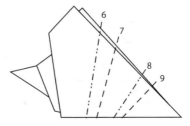

3 Inside-reverse all four of the folds, two on each side, corresponding to the angles shown. Now pre-crease along the folds marked 6, 7, 8, and 9, and then inside-reverse these folds.

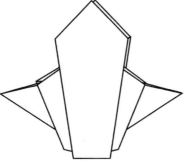

4 Here is the completed flower wrap, Hana Tsutsumi.

NOSHI AWABI

Traditional design demonstrated by Greg Mudarri

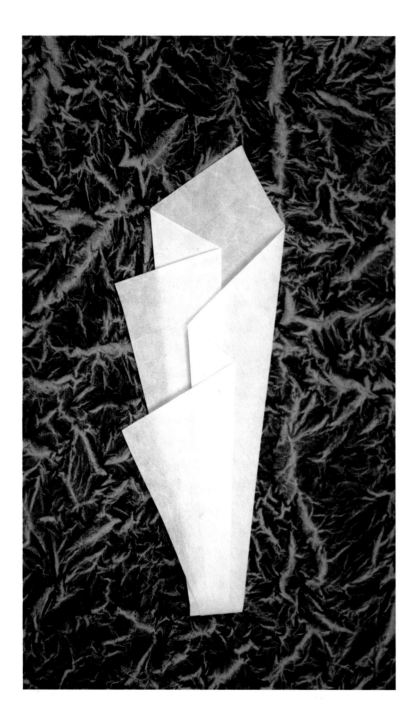

This is the original noshi that was folded to present the gift of dried abalone. Use a paper that is roughly letter size, though all the folds are approximate and could be produced from nearly any size rectangle. On the diagrams, arrows are left out for clarity. Pay attention to the proportions and the shapes, and practice with inexpensive papers, opening to compare your crease placements with the drawings as you master these patterns.

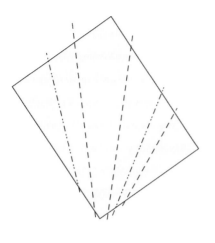

1 This is the Noshi Awabi crease pattern, which features only five folds.

2 Make a diagonal-fold from a point close to the lower corner. The left corner will touch the right side.

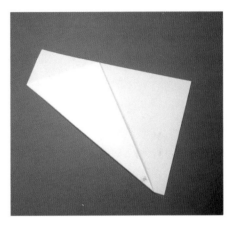

3 Make a valley fold, placing the corner outside the previous fold.

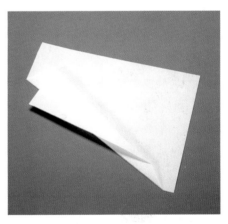

4 Make another diagonal fold from a point near the bottom corner, much like the first fold. (See step 5.)

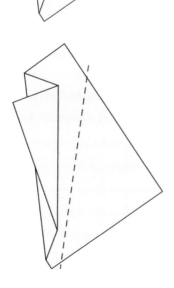

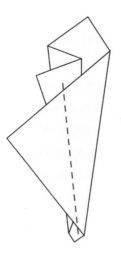

5 Valley-fold again to let the corner pass outside the previous fold, this time farther than before.

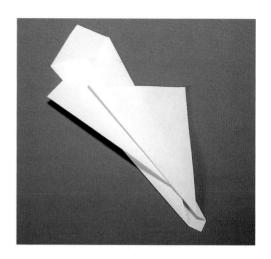

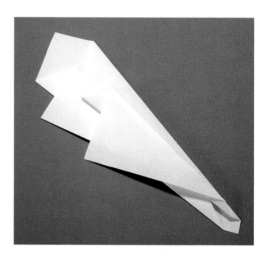

6 Valley-fold to bring the corner across the opposite side. Try to echo the shape of the corner above. (See step 7.)

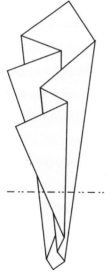

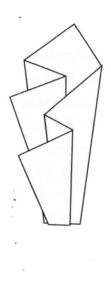

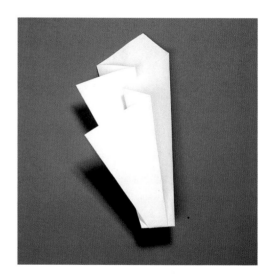

7 Mountain-fold the bottom behind. Be sure to let the under-layers show on both sides of the uppermost layer.

8 This is the completed Noshi Awabi. Notice how the shapes relate in a pleasing manner without rigid construction.

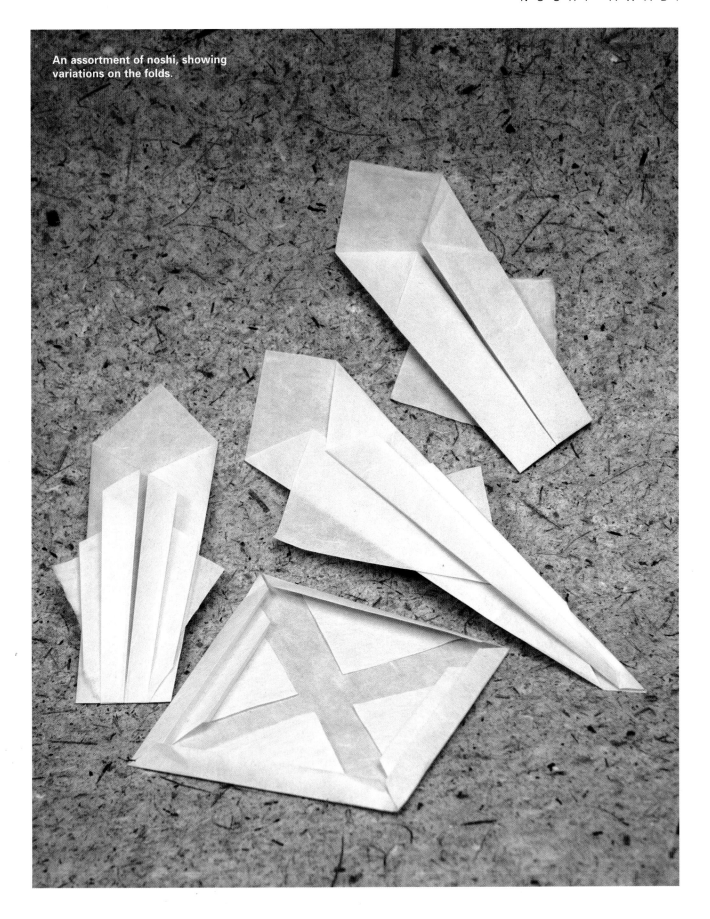

An assortment of noshi, showing
variations on the folds.

CELEBRATED FRIENDSHIPS

Sailboat Envelope ■ *Masu Box*

Wallet or Clutch Purse ■ *Crane's Egg Modular Box*

SAILBOAT ENVELOPE

Designed and demonstrated by Michael G. LaFosse

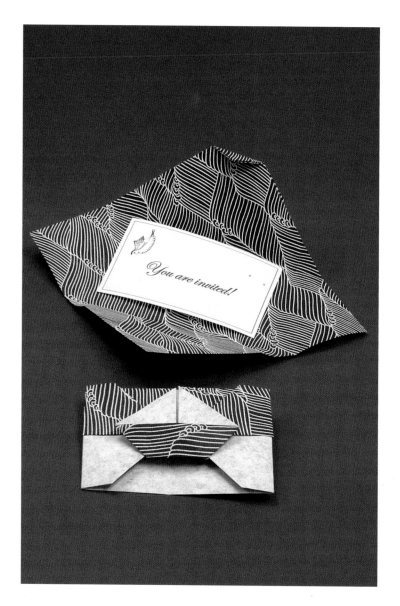

Envelopes folded from beautiful washi will greatly enhance your invitations, thank-you notes, and special congratulatory messages, making them keepsakes suitable for framing. Use a 10-inch (25cm) square of washi that is white on one side, such as chiyogami, for an envelope that will measure 3 ½ inches by 5 ¼ inches (9cm by 13cm).

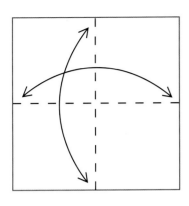

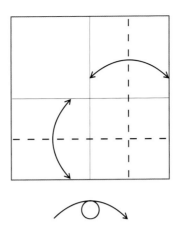

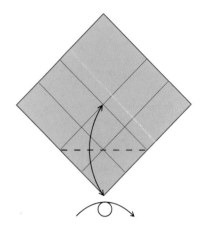

1 Begin white side up, then fold in half, edge to opposite edge. Then open, rotate, and repeat, forming crossing creases.

2 Fold bottom edge to center horizontal crease, and unfold. Repeat with the right edge. Turn the model over.

3 Observe the crease pattern, and then orient your paper as shown. Fold bottom corner to the center, and unfold. Turn model over.

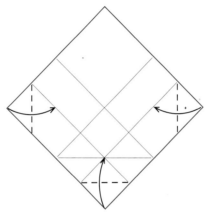

4 Your paper should look like this.

5 Fold the three corners inward to the crease lines as shown.

6 Tuck the adjacent flaps inward and over the white side of the paper, forming a triangular hull with two white triangular sails. The tips of the sails will meet at the center of the original square.

7 Lay the model flat. Burnish the creases with a folding tool, such as a bone folder.

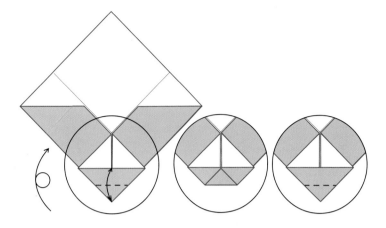

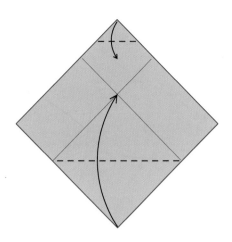

8 Fold the bottom, colored corner up to touch the middle of the sailboat shape, and unfold. Flip the model over, from bottom to top.

9 Using the crease made in step 8, fold the top corner down. Fold the bottom corner up to where the creases cross.

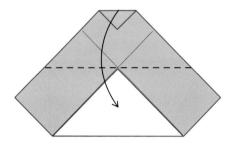

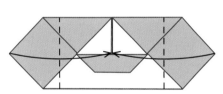

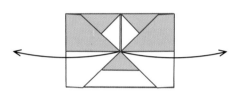

10 Fold down the top part of the model at the place where the creases cross. Look ahead at step 11 for the correct shape.

11 Fold the left and right corners to the middle.

12 Bring the corners back to their original position.

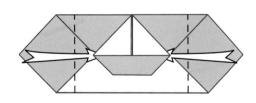

13 Tuck the side corners under the ends of the sailboat.

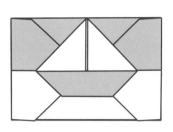

14 Your finished Sailboat Envelope!

15 Open the envelope. Make an invitation card to fit the rectangle defined by the four valley folds.

16 This wave-inspired washi pattern makes a wonderful Sailboat Envelope. Go buy a boat, and then invite all your friends to help you sail it! Who could possibly turn down such an invitation?

MASU BOX

Traditional design demonstrated by Michael G. LaFosse

The *masu*, or "measuring box," is one of the most useful origami models, but most people only fold square boxes, which are not always the most practical or beautiful. Washi boxes are timeless, and they are always welcome gifts. They can be made to nest for storage and then be brought out for use during special occasions. This method allows you to customize the dimensions of your box, the only limit being the size of the washi paper you choose. This clean and simple shape beautifully displays quality washi, and you can also modify the proportions to complement the patterns and shapes of the washi itself. Do not be intimidated by the initial measuring steps. Once you do it, you will realize how easy it is to create a template that you will use to quickly create more of your favorite boxes and lids as you discover even more wonderful papers.

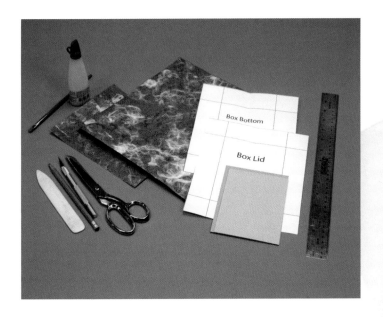

Materials

- Washi
- Glue or acrylic paste
- Fiberboard
- Template paper

Equipment

- Straight edge
- Blade or scissors
- Glue brush
- Folding tool (bone folder, back of a spoon, or something similar)
- Pencil

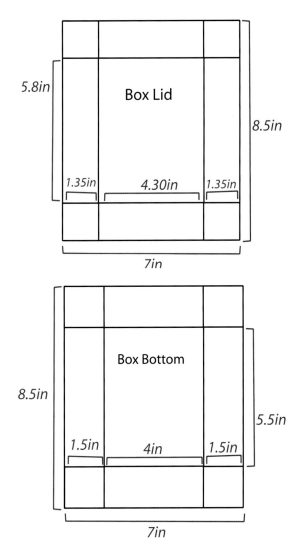

1 Make a template like the one shown in the diagram, by first creating a rectangle with the desired length and width of your box, centered as shown. Now expand the rectangle by adding an even margin all around the outside of the rectangle. This width represents the desired height (or depth) of the box. This decorative paper will become the lid. Use the same procedure to make another box template to form the inner box (bottom), but this time, draw it slightly smaller in length and width, about ¼ inch (6mm) smaller each way, but this also depends on the thickness of the paper you choose.

Perhaps you will choose to cut the base from a different, complementary color of paper. If you wish the lower portion of the inner box to show beneath the lid (for easier opening) make the smaller box slightly deeper by increasing the size of the margin drawn around the center rectangle drawn for the inner box.

Select sheets of washi that will be large enough to allow the templates to fit when rotated 45 degrees about their center. Trim the paper so the sides just touch each edge of the expanded rectangle template, noting that this will leave four right triangles of excess paper between each side of the rectangular template and each corner of the washi. Here we are using a template that is 8½ inches by 7 inches (22cm by 18cm). This size template will fit into an 11-inch (28cm) square. Calculate the size of washi square that will accommodate your template by adding two adjacent sides of your template, then dividing by 1.414. For example: 8.5 + 7 = 15.5 inches; 15.5 ÷ 1.414 = 10.96 inches (or 11 inches).

2 Lightly draw the diagonals (ghost lines) on the back side of the washi.

3 Align the center folds of the template onto the diagonal marks on the washi. Transfer all measurements from the template by making pencil marks on the back of the washi.

4 Use a straight edge to firmly mark the washi all the way across corresponding to the inner and outer lines of the template. Press firmly, effectively scoring the washi for easier folding.

5 Fold all corner flaps inward as shown. Notice how one pair of opposite corners overlaps but the other pair of opposite corners do not meet.

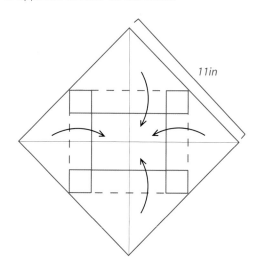

11in

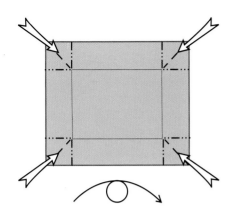

6 Make the box walls by folding the outer edges inward, as shown. Use the previously scored crease lines. Turn the model over.

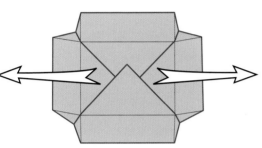

7 Pinch the corners closed by folding along each of the ends of the outer rectangle (the box depth indication lines).

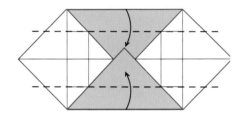

8 The box forms. Pull out the indicated corners, left and right.

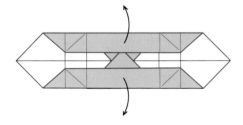

9 Fold the top and bottom edges inward as shown. Raise them perpendicular to the table, forming vertical side walls.

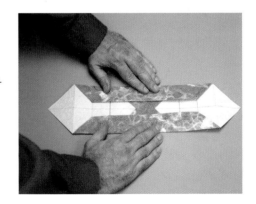

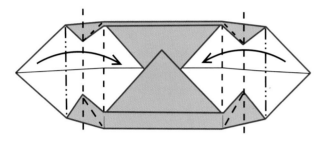
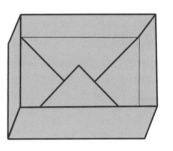

10 Using the creases, close the end of the box by tucking the corners inside. Repeat on the other end.

11 Cut a rectangular piece of fiberboard to fit within the center rectangle of the template. When covered, this will insert inside the box, stiffening the lid. Cut a piece of washi large enough to allow you to completely cover one side and all four edges. Allow for about a ½-inch (1cm) overlap at each edge on the back of the board. Trim the corners as shown. Apply paste to one side of the board, then to the edges of the washi. Align the centers and fold the excess washi over the edges of the board.

12 Paste or glue sparingly, so as not to pucker the outer layer of washi. Insert the board into the box.

13 Use the slightly smaller template to make a smaller box in the same way (shown, sized to fit inside the fancy paper box). The red washi box becomes the lid.

14 Here is the completed rectangular masu box. Try several patterns and sizes. Who would not want to make a washi box for every precious thing?

WALLET OR CLUTCH PURSE

Designed and demonstrated by Michael G. LaFosse

This wallet or clutch purse is a great way for you to take your favorite washi out on the town, where others can enjoy it too. A person's taste in elegant papers is not unlike their taste in fashion, and you may have a perfect outfit to go with a special piece of paper. Perhaps you have already made earrings from the Crane's Egg Modular Box design (see page 88), and you need a clutch purse to complete the ensemble. When you make them yourself, you know that your accessories are not only handmade but also one-of-a-kind!

Materials

- Washi
- Fabric
- Thermal bonding film or iron-set fusible web
- Heavy thread
- White glue (not shown)

Equipment

- Sewing needle
- Scissors
- Straight edge
- Folding tool (bone folder, back of a spoon, or something similar)
- Awl or small hole punch (not shown)
- Iron and ironing board (not shown)
- Glue brush (not shown)

1 Gather your materials. Select thin fabric and thick thread in colors that complement the chosen washi. Various thermal bonding films allow backing the washi with fabric, using a dry mount press or a hand iron and ironing board.

2 Cut the fabric width to match the final, desired width of the wallet. The wallet shown is 9 inches (23cm) wide and 4 inches (10cm) tall. Cut the fabric length to six times the desired height plus ½ inch (1cm), to allow for a ¼-inch (6mm) hem at each end, top and bottom. Our example is 24 inches (61cm) long. Cut the washi ½ inch (1cm) longer and wider than the desired dimensions to allow a ¼-inch (6mm) hem for the long sides. (The washi will be folded over to finish the edge of the purse, so no exposed fabric edges will unravel.)

Bond the backs of the washi and fabric together by trimming the bonding film to the size of the fabric, then laying it on the back of the washi so that all exposed margins are equal. (Be sure your hot iron does not directly contact any thermal bonding film. Follow the manufacturer's recommendations for temperature and time.)

3 Trim the corners of the washi to the tip of the fabric, so that layers will not build up as you fold the margins back (as the hem).

4 Apply white glue to the exposed margins of washi and allow it to dry to a tacky state before folding the hem over to seal. Fold the edges over, then burnish well with a folding tool. Allow the glue or paste to dry. Place under a weighted board for added pressure if necessary; use waxed paper to prevent glue from sticking to the board.

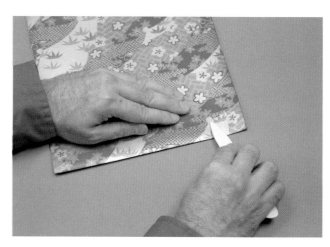

5 Here is the finished washi-fabric composite, ready for use.

6 Fold the rectangle in half, short edge to short edge.

7 Fold this again, this time into equal thirds. Crease by pinching in the center first. Always fold from the center to the edges.

8 Flatten, and then crease well.

9 Open the folded rectangle. Close the fourth panel over the third (counting from the left).

10 Panels three and four are hidden.

11 Fold the bottom panel up and burnish.

12 Using an awl, punch small holes along each edge for stitches. Space the holes evenly, but make the holes at the top and bottom closer to the ends, so that the stitching will hold the layers tightly together at the corners. Coordinate the numbers and placement of the holes according to the pattern or design on the paper.

13 Using heavyweight thread and a needle, stitch the panels of the wallet together, securing each end with sturdy knots. This particular type of stitch also binds the edges (as it does in the Sewn-Bound Washi Book project on page 120).

14 Fold over the top left corner of the open flap. Make the side edge parallel to the lower edge and allow a space of approximately ½ inch (1cm).

15 Fold the opposite corner across the first, forming a point at the top, as shown.

16 Tuck the rest of the flap beneath the upper layer, to finish the edge. The off-centered corner is easy to handle. (Left-handed people will want to fold the mirror image of these last few steps.)

17 Fold the flap over the front . . .

. . . and then crease.

18 To close the wallet, just tuck the folded flap inside the pocket at the base.

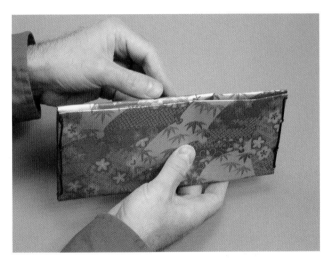

19 Here is a bottom or back view of the closed wallet.

20 Here is a top or front view of the closed wallet.

CRANE'S EGG MODULAR BOX

Designed by Richard L. Alexander and demonstrated by Michael G. LaFosse

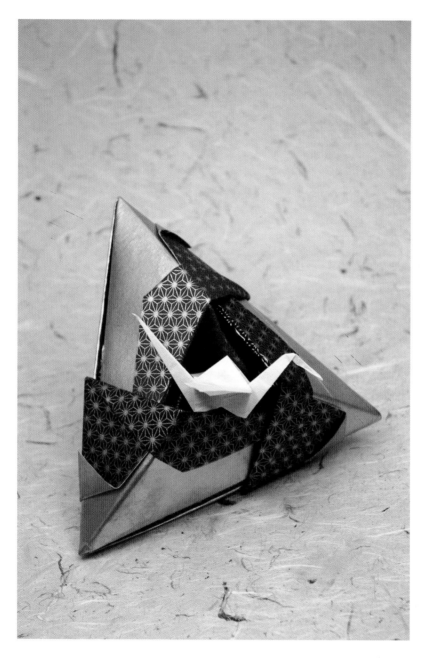

This modular box can be a useful table decoration, vessel, gift box, or hanging ornament. The model is infinitely variable. It shows off both sides of the washi, so it is a great model to fold from "duo" (or two-color) papers, or sheets of colorful washi bonded back-to-back (see the back-coating instructions on page 46). When made small, these modular forms make distinctive earrings. When made large, they can be used to decorate holiday tables.

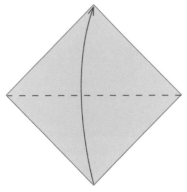

1 Begin with three sheets of square paper, all the same size. Fold each of the three squares in half to form this triangular shape. The side showing will become the outer corners of the Crane's Egg. The photos show inexpensive, duo origami paper for clarity.

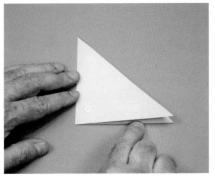

2 Fold the triangle in half, and then open it back to the larger triangle. Repeat all steps with the other two pieces. Turn the model over.

3 This is the orientation with the right angle pointing toward you and the centerline ridge (mountain fold) facing up.

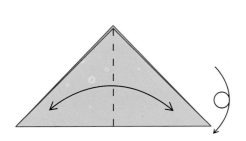

4 Fold the tip of the right angle (only the top layer of paper) up to the center of the folded diagonal. (This is the flap that can be varied to produce an infinite number of decorative faces.)

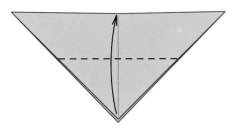

5 Fold up each of the two cut edges of the indicated layer, so that each edge is parallel to the top edge. (The two folds meet at the centerline.)

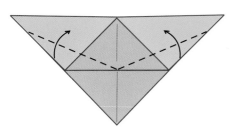

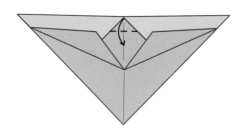

6 Fold the top corner down, so the tip touches an imaginary line connecting the two edges shown in step 5.

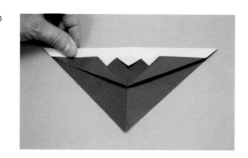

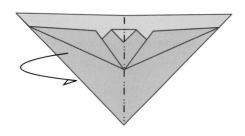

7 Re-crease the centerline, folding the paper in half as shown.

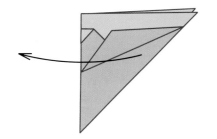

8 Open.

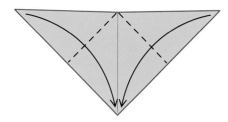

9 Fold the corners from each side down to meet at the lowest corner in the center. Crease sharply.

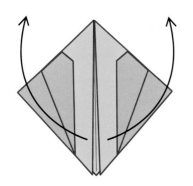

10 Open each flap to form right angles at the left and right valley creases. Restore the center fold to cup the shape, so the two side angles come together, forming the shape of a party hat.

11 Here is the completed element.

12 Insert each of the narrow corners at the split end into a pocket on the front of another piece. (Keep the tops of the party hats pointing out. Keep the narrow corners out until they can be inserted into the pockets of another piece.) Insert the third piece into the second in the same manner.

13 Finally, bring the corners from the first piece around, and tuck each one into respective pockets of the last piece.

14 Here is the finished Crane's Egg Modular Box.

15 To open the Crane's Egg Modular Box, simply squeeze the poles.

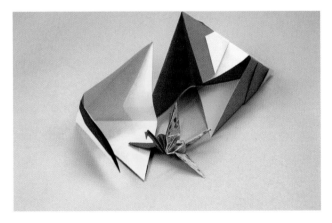

These twin cranes feel right at home next to this egg!

PERSONALIZED SPACES

Tato ■ *Vase Cover* ■ *Desktop Organizer*
"Ceramic" Form with Chirigi-e ■ *Tulip Bowl*
Hurricane Bowl ■ *Sewn-Bound Washi Book*

TATO

Traditional design demonstrated by Michael G. LaFosse

The *tato* (pronounced *tah toe*) is a pleated coin purse. Numerous designs have been developed by origami artists, and more durable tatos are often folded from leather when used for coins. The purse opens like a flower when you pull it from two opposite points. Colorful washi tatos make excellent holders for small items, such as stamps and coins, and they can be quite elaborate. This simple design is one you can make from your favorite washi. Use it daily, give it to a friend, mail it, or simply enjoy it as a decorative way to keep small, precious items.

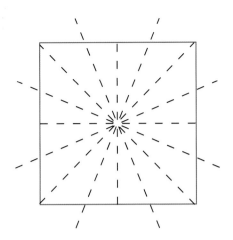

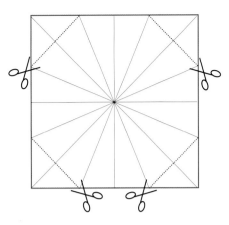

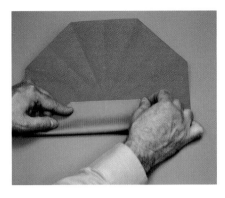

1 Use a square piece of washi, 10 to 12 inches (25 to 30cm). Divide it into sixteen wedges, like this: Begin by folding it in half diagonally each way and then edgewise each way (eighths). Complete the divisions by folding in half between all existing creases. (Line up one crease over its adjacent crease, fold, and repeat. All of the creases go through the center point.)

2 Cut each of the corners as indicated to create a regular octagon.

3 Place the bottom edge along the centerline.

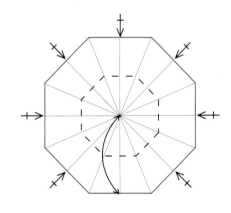

4 Fold between the indicated creases. Unfold. Repeat with all other edges.

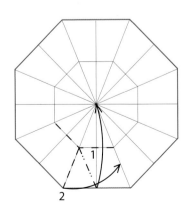

5 Begin to close the purse by refolding each edge to the center (step 1). Move the corner inward (step 2) and flatten.

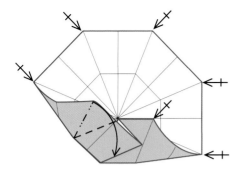

6 Repeat with each corner, working your way around. We have worked clockwise, as shown.

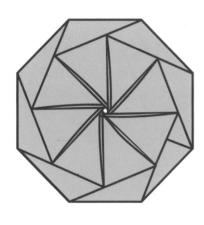

7 Open the shape to allow you to complete folding the last corners.

8 Gather all of the corners and edges inward.

9 Flatten to close, making sure all points lay in the same direction.

10 Here is the completed washi tato.

11 To create a decorative, two-colored trim, open the tato and turn it upside down.

12 Fold each outside corner inward, as shown.

13 Turn over and re-close the tato.

VASE COVER

Designed and demonstrated by Michael G. LaFosse

This project introduces a simple way to construct a workable, shapeable washi composite with a watercolor core. With this technique, East meets West to provide a whole new, three-dimensional life for your most wonderful washi.

Covering otherwise mundane shapes, such as glass vases, with washi can make a beautiful home even more stunning. This washi vase cover is easy to make, versatile, and elegant. When dry, the vase cover is a springy coil and can be used to hug a variety of different vase sizes and shapes. (Look ahead at the photos to see how this works.) Why store a cabinet full of glass vases? With these washi covers you'll only need one vase! Make several; they nest for storage.

Materials

- Two sheets of washi: one decorative and one for a lining
- One rectangle of watercolor paper
- Glue or paste

Equipment

- Spray bottle of water
- Scissors (not shown)
- Glue brush (China Bristle), 3″ (8cm) wide
- Dish for glue
- Sharp blade (optional)

1 Gather your materials. Determine the size of paper by considering the size of the vase or container you want to cover. The rectangle's length should be twice the widest circumference of the vase, and the rectangle's width should be at least as tall as the vase. Trim the sheets so that the outer, more decorative paper is about ½ inch (1cm) larger in each dimension than the rectangles of watercolor and the liner washi.

2 Using the spray bottle, moisten each of the pieces until each feels soft but not wet.

3 Use the brush to evenly apply a layer of glue to the back of the largest, most decorative rectangle, working it from the center to the edges.

4 Lay the smaller rectangle of white watercolor paper squarely onto the pasted back of the decorative washi.

5 Apply glue to the back of the watercolor paper to accept the next layer of washi. Fold over the excess, decorative paper from the bottom layer to finish the edges. Apply more paste to the decorative margins.

6 Lay the moistened, lining washi squarely onto the pasted surface, and press gently.

7 Here is the finished composite of washi/watercolor paper core/washi, ready to use. It can be formed now, or left to dry completely, and then rewetted for later shaping.

8 While the washi composite is moist, wrap it into the form of a tapered cylinder. You may also wrap it around a glass vase or even a wine bottle. Leave the top slightly more open, so that you can easily place or remove the insert.

9 Secure the form with strips of leftover watercolor paper as shown. Allow to dry completely before removing the restraining strips.

10 To set the coil in an exact position or angle, you may want to secure the shape with an optional slit: Using a sharp blade, create a slit just long enough to accept one corner from the outside of the coil.

11 Tuck the corner into the slit as shown. This method of securing the form allows it to remain adjustable.

12 Insert a suitable container, and let the vase cover dry completely. (Be sure to choose a waterproof container if you will be adding cut flowers.)

13 Here is the finished washi Vase Cover.

DESKTOP ORGANIZER
(PEN/PENCIL/BRUSH HOLDER)

Designed and demonstrated by Michael G. LaFosse

Your workspace is a reflection of your personality. So many desk furnishings are boring and bland; why not spruce them up with your favorite washi colors, textures, and patterns cleverly applied to useful forms? These handy desk organizer forms are quick and easy to make, so making several allows you to change them with the seasons and holidays. These modular elements can be easily nested when stored, then combined in creative ways to keep your work area fresh and exciting with useful, personalized sculpture. (The form shown can also be used as a decorative vase cover.)

Materials

- Desk organizer cups or favorite shapes you want to cover
- Washi
- Watercolor paper
- Glue or paste

Equipment

- Spray bottle of water
- Scissors
- Glue brush (China Bristle), 3″ (8cm) wide
- Dish for glue

1 Begin with a watercolor-core composite (see Vase Cover project on page 97 for construction details). The project shown is made from a long, tapering trapezoid, but you may want to relate the shape of your form to the washi you have chosen.

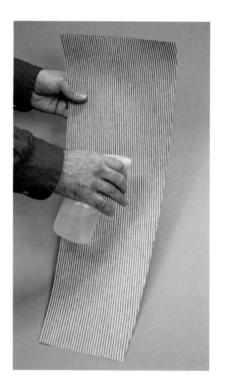

2 Moisten the composite if it has dried.

3 Form a double coil, with each end rolled from opposite directions, resulting in two cylinders.

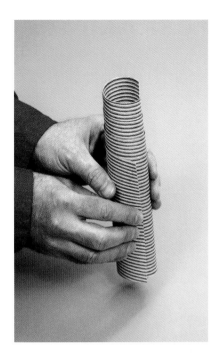

4 Here is the side view of the coiled piece. Restrain and secure the form with clips or strips of paper until completely dry.

5 Use another, shorter or longer strip to create a third cylinder, which will be attached by insertion after it has dried.

6 Roll tightly into the form of a cylinder, with the shortest edge on the outside, and secure it as before. Allow it to dry completely.

7 Unroll the single cylinder just enough to insert the outside edge into the coil between the two cylinders of the double-cylinder form.

8 Here is the finished Desktop Organizer. Insert a cylindrical liner, such as a tall plastic glass or cup, or a suitable can. (Save a narrow, cylindrical plastic container from your drink concentrates and powders.) The liners will protect your desk and the washi from ink pen or pencil points.

"CERAMIC" FORM WITH CHIGIRI-E

Designed and demonstrated by Michael G. LaFosse and Richard L. Alexander

This versatile style of "pottery" uses no kiln and no glazes, and it creates no hazardous emissions! Products such as Celuclay are mixtures of finely shredded paper (processed almost to a powder) and binding agents that react with water to form a hard but lightweight mass of cellulose when dry. As workable as clay, it is widely used in papier mache projects. This product allows the artist to make lightweight objects of any shape and size quickly and easily.

This project demonstrates an art form the Japanese call chigiri-e, or "torn paper pictures," enabling the artist to use the infinite palette of colors and textures of washi in ways that cannot be done by selecting only a sheet or two. Here is a perfect chance to showcase even the smallest scraps of your favorite washi, setting them off in a completely different context. A piece of deep blue washi reminded me of a mountain lake, so now a small scrap of this favorite paper becomes that pristine pool! You, the artist, are in control of the shapes, shadows, and even the mass of the washi you choose to honor through your art.

Materials

- Washi of your choice (not shown)

- Celuclay powder mixture (available from most national art supply chain stores and catalog houses)

- Aluminum foil (or waxed paper)

- Glue or paste (not shown)

- Water

Equipment

- Rolling pin, thick wood dowel, or pipe

- Boards (as thick as you want your slabs to be)

- Mixing bowl

- Butter knife (not shown)

- Dinner fork (not shown)

- Paper and pencil, or computer (for making shape templates) (not shown)

- Dust mask (not shown)

- Glue brush (not shown)

- Coarse sandpaper

1 Gently add water to the powder in a bowl. (When working with any dusty material, always wear a dust mask. Consider working outdoors, or under a ventilation fan.)

2 Knead and add water until the dough is a uniform and workable consistency.

3 Pat the dough into a shallow trough lined with the aluminum foil, backed on the sides with the boards. (You may choose to bring the foil up the sides of the wood, if the foil is wide enough. This will prevent the dough from sticking to the wood.) The thickness of your slab will be controlled by the thickness of the boards you choose. We often use leftover strips of thick foamcore.

4 Cover the dough with another piece of aluminum foil.

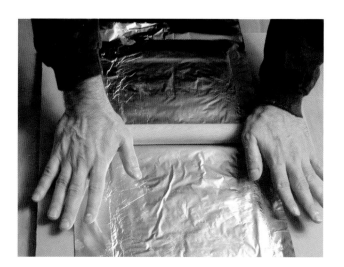

5 Roll the slab evenly between the aluminum foil as the sides are contained within the boards. Work the excess dough to one end or the other of the trough.

6 Remove the aluminum foil to reveal the dough slab of uniform thickness.

7 Allow the slab to set or rest for a few hours (more or less, depending on the temperature and humidity). After it is firm, but not dry, lay out the templates for your chosen design. This example will be a rustic, nearly square vase with rounded corners. This shape was easy to make on a computer. Just print, and then cut out the shapes from regular printer paper.

8 These are long, uniform strips we will use as the side walls of the vase. The "volcano" form on the left will be my bottle's neck. These components need a few more hours to dry before they are sufficiently firm to handle. (You can also control the drying time. Covering the material with plastic will retard the drying if you must leave for an extended period.)

9 Score (roughen) the edges with a dinner fork while the dough is fairly easy to work (before the pieces dry too much). This will help ensure good contact when the pieces are joined.

10 Install the vertical walls, smoothing the seams to ensure good contact between the pieces.

11 Remove enough material at the top side to accommodate the neck. Allow all of the pieces to dry, making sure they are quite firm before you assemble them.

12 Mix, form, and then apply a thin rope of moist dough to the edges of the side walls. The other slab side will be placed on top of the rope.

13 Place the other side wall on the moist rope. Smooth the seams as before. Notice that the side slab is stiff.

14 Affix the neck over the hole. Use moist dough to fill any gaps. You may also attach it with glue if the fit is snug enough. When completely dry, the vase can be smoothed, carved, sanded, or worked in a multitude of ways, depending on your vision of the final product. I want mine to be primitive, because the washi that I selected is earthy, with bits of unprocessed plant fiber.

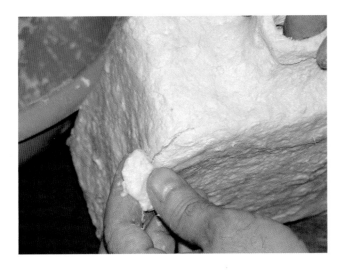

15 With moist dough, patch any cracks that may appear during drying.

16 Shape with coarse sandpaper. Smooth as desired.

17 Apply torn patches of washi with glue, creating your own picture. It helps to moisten the paper where you want to tear it.

18 Here is the finished "ceramic" form, a chigiri-e vase!

TULIP BOWL

Designed by Richard L. Alexander and demonstrated by Greg Mudarri

his Tulip Bowl demonstrates how you can impart whatever qualities and strengths you need into the washi with simple composite construction techniques. Richard designed this origami tulip for a field of paper flowers in twelve retail store windows (Saks Fifth Avenue in New York City). Unlike the traditional origami tulip design (which is folded from a blintzed preliminary form), his is a more dynamic design—a tulip with a twist. This design also allowed us to efficiently pack hundreds of prefolded blossoms by nesting one inside the next. Since his design has a flat base, it also works beautifully as a bowl when made from a large enough square. This project demonstrates how to incorporate stiffness into an object that would otherwise be too structurally weak to use as a bowl. It also shows how it can be fun to respect the printed pattern and incorporate it into the shape and style of the piece. Here we have trimmed the edge along the washi's printed, scalloped line for a distinctive and pleasing effect.

Materials

- Two sheets of washi—select colors that complement one another, because one will be the outer surface and one will line the bowl
- Aluminum mesh window screen
- Adhesive, glue, paste, or thermal bonding film (not shown)

Equipment

- Scissors or shears to cut the screen and paper
- Straight edge to aid in trimming the paper square
- Thermal dry mount press, or iron and ironing board (not shown)

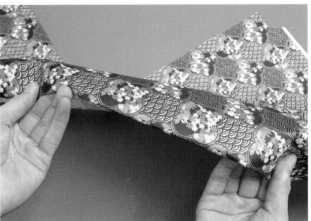

1 Consider how the top edge of your bowl would best relate to the washi design. Our sample lends itself to a scalloped edge.

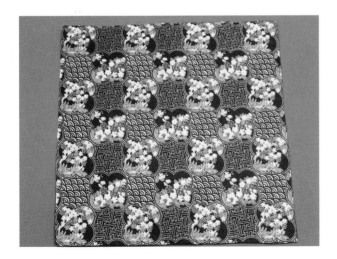

2 Cut the washi square. The bowl's height will be half the length of the original square, or 5 inches (13cm) high if you start from a 10-inch (25cm) square. The widest distance across the bowl (diagonally) will be 7½ inches (19cm).

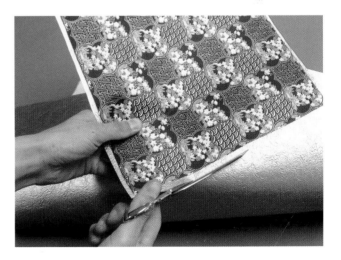

3 Cut the lining paper square. Leave a margin so that it is a little larger than the washi square.

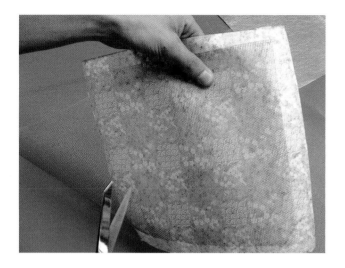

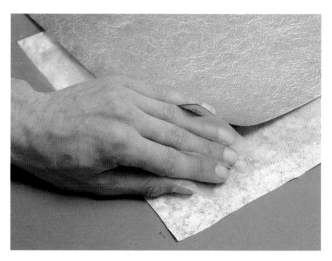

4 Cut the aluminum screen square, but make it about an inch smaller than the paper squares, for a good seal between the papers without the possibility of any sharp protrusions of wire at the edges.

5 Stack the squares in this order (from the top): Front side of the lining washi, thermal bonding film, aluminum screen, thermal bonding film, back of outer washi.

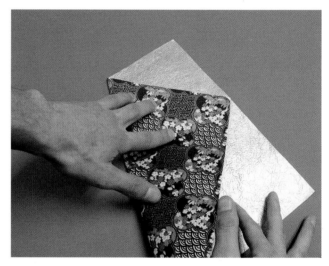

6 Align the centers and corners, and then heat with a hand iron or a dry mount press. Trim the resulting composite (the bonded layers of washi with aluminum mesh sandwiched between). This is the back of the trimmed composite, showing the gold washi we selected for the lining of the bowl.

7 Fold the lower corner over to the opposite side on the right. Adjust the point along the edge until you define two isosceles triangles in the backing color, on either side of the corner you brought across. After you are fairly sure that the two shorter sides of each triangle are equal, crease the composite. Trust your eye. There is no need to measure, because this step is self-correcting!

8 Open, rotate the sheet counter-clockwise 90 degrees, and then fold the crease back onto itself, touching the new corner of the square to the upper right-hand side while making sure the next corner (shown at the top) is also an isosceles triangle. This imparts a crease exactly perpendicular to your first crease. Open. Rotate the sheet again, and crease again for each corner, and then open. As you repeat this with the other corners, each of the creases will align with themselves. When opened, the pattern forms a rotated "tic-tac-toe" board.

9 All of the pre-creases are in place. Note the rotated square in the center, formed by the intersecting pairs of parallel valley folds.

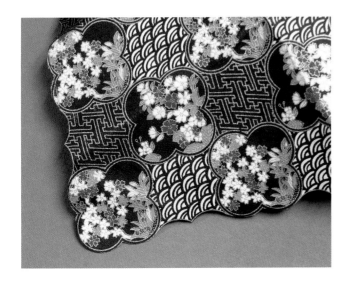

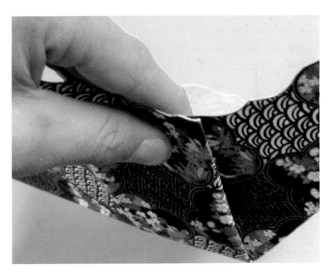

10 If you want to trim the edge, do so after the pre-creasing is completed, just in case the washi layers shift while creasing. (We have cut along the pattern to form a scalloped edge.)

11 Collapse the bowl at each side by pushing the top edge near each corner, inward and to the left, aligning the corner edge with the doubled-back inside edge of the bowl. Pinch the layers together, forming a mountain fold from the corner of the rotated box at the center when the cut (top) edges of the bowl align.

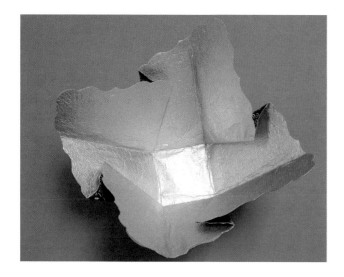

12 This pinch forms a dart on each corner of the bowl. This is the top view before darts are locked into place.

13 Roll the upper corner of each doubled layer behind the dart (inside the bowl) to lock it in place. Each locked dart is five thicknesses of composite!

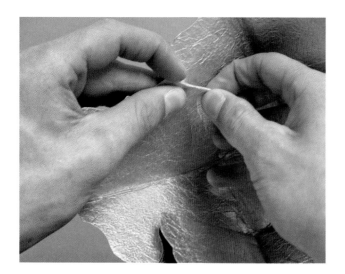

14 Pinch firmly to crimp the aluminum screen mesh inside the composite. (For larger bowls requiring stiffer mesh, use a mallet to set the dart locks.)

15 Here is the completed washi Tulip Bowl.

HURRICANE BOWL

Designed and demonstrated by Michael G. LaFosse

One of the most intriguing things to me is how a flat plane transforms into a spectacular form with just a simple cut and twist. This bowl will show off your favorite washi by incorporating bold lines and curves to accent the colors. Your ultimate needs will dictate how much reinforcement will be required. Washi backed with watercolor paper is quite stiff, but a fruit bowl may require back-coating to a piece of wood veneer or even a plastic laminate. In this instance, you may also want to back the other side of the bowl. Begin with a stiffly back-coated square of washi. Decide which washi you want to feature on the inside of the bowl.

Materials

- Square of back-coated washi or composite

Equipment

- Scissors
- Straight edge
- Glue or paste
- Glue brush
- Compass, or round dish to serve as a template
- Small spring clips or spring-type clothespins
- Pencil

1 Measure the length of the square. Mark each midpoint. Multiply the length by 0.667 to determine the diameter of a circle (measuring two-thirds of the length of the square). Using a pencil, draw the circle on the underside of the washi, so it intersects the side of the square at the midpoint. If you have a dish with a diameter close to two-thirds of the square, it will serve as a useful template and save time.

2 Repeat until all four circles each intersect their side of the square at their midpoints.

3 Using a straight edge and a pencil, describe a smaller square area around the center of the paper, with its corners at the four points where adjacent circles intersect.

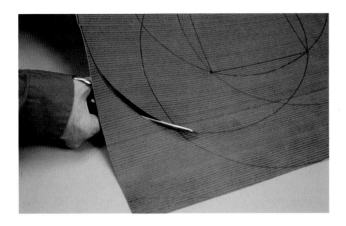

4 Begin to cut along a circle in only one direction, from the center of a side.

5 Rotate and cut through the next circle, cutting in the same direction, but stop at the corner of the inner square. Repeat this at each side of the square piece of washi.

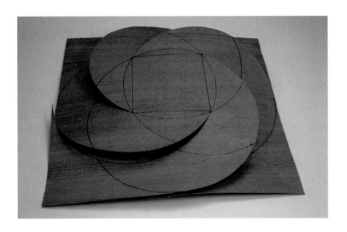

6 Cutting is complete. The bowl center has been popped up to show the resulting form.

7 This is the back side, popped up. Note that the busier pattern obscures the cut lines.

8 Apply glue to the portion of the tip that will contact the adjacent flap.

9 Align the two curved edges of cut paper, then slide the glued point to the desired position, and then clamp with a small spring clip. Using the same alignment, repeat at each of the four sides.

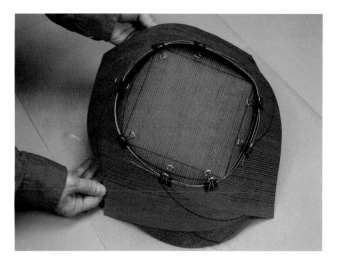

10 Small spring clips allow the glued flaps to dry in place.

11 Remove the clips after the glue has dried. The reinforced rim circumscribes the bottom of the square base.

12 The inside of the finished bowl is awash with flying cranes.

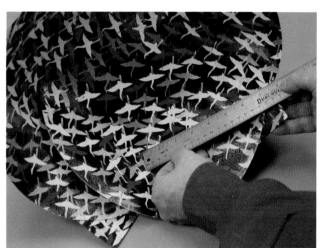

13 If your washi has a busy pattern, as this does, why not set off the curved shapes of the cuts by inserting complementary arcs of composite? Just measure the straight line distance (cord) across the curved part of the bowl that shows. Then make or find a template (such as a dish with the same diameter as two-thirds of your original square), and use it to cut four arcs from pieces of leftover washi composite. The arcs' straight line distance (cord) must match the measurement.

14 Lay the dish or template onto the edge of the scrap composite to match the length of the cord. Mark along the edge of the template, and then cut out four.

15 Paste and insert the new arcs upside down, between the curved lips to accentuate the shapes of the curves with the back color showing on the inside of the bowl.

16 Here is the finished washi Hurricane Bowl.

SEWN-BOUND WASHI BOOK

Traditional design demonstrated by Michael G. LaFosse

Even though more people have probably tried writing books than have tried making them, it is much easier to make a book than to write one! People say, "Don't judge a book by its cover"; however, often we *do* judge books by their covers, and washi makes not only distinctive covers but exceptional pages.

The design of this book allows you to print directly onto the washi and then fold the pages for a doubled thickness. This prevents the printing from showing through the delicate washi, and it makes the exposed edges of the book more durable because they are all folded. Traditionally, printing was transferred to the page by pressing the paper against an inked woodblock, so folded pages were common: Woodblock printing is best done on only one side of a sheet; a two-sided printed page is accomplished by a fold in the middle of the sheet, forming back-to-back printing.

If you plan to use the book as an heirloom or treasured keepsake, other small mementos, such as photos, can be inserted between the pages of this book without contacting the printing.

Materials

- Washi (momigami works great for the front and back covers)

- Good-quality, natural color Kozo, Mitsumata, or Gampi fiber paper for the pages of the book

- Thread (carpet thread or binder's linen threads are of suitable weight)

- Glue or paste

Equipment

- Needle (an upholstery needle or book binder's needle works best)

- Scissors

- Straight edge

- Carpenter's square

- Folding tool

- Awl (or other small hole punch)

- Glue brush

- Computer and printer

1 Gather everything you will need for whatever size book you desire. Be sure to allow an extra inch of paper for edge overlap when selecting your washi for the covers. When selecting the washi for the book's text pages, remember that each page will be doubled, so be sure to purchase or make enough.

2 Look carefully at both sides of the paper that you will use for your pages: The side of the sheet that was in contact with the drying surface will be smooth and even; the other side will probably have a slightly rougher texture, and you may be able to see marks made by the brush used to apply the sheet to the drying surface. For a crisp image, it is best to print only on the smooth side of the paper. After printing, the washi is folded in half to produce a page that appears to be printed front and back, with the page's outside edge actually being the *folded* edge.

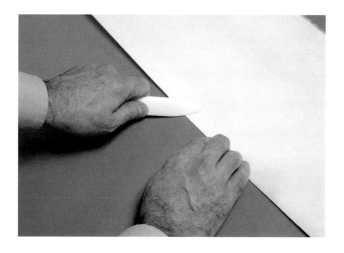

3 Fold the washi in half, smooth side out. Use a folding tool to burnish the crease.

4 Cut the pages to the desired height, making sure that height will fit through your printer. We have trimmed off the deckle edges.

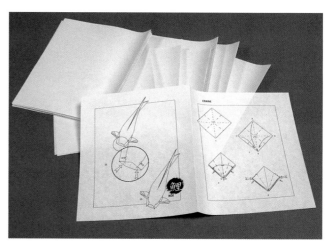

5 Load your washi into a sheet-fed printer. This one is an ink-jet printer. (A laser printer can be used, but note that it won't work as well on washi that is soft and fuzzy.)

6 Notice that the printed image appears on the side of the sheet with the mountain crease. Your pages may be printed, or left blank for journal entries, stories, poems, or notes. Blank books also make great gifts as scrapbooks, photo albums, and diaries. They can be made any size, because they do not need to be inserted into a printer.

7 Cut the cover to size. My cover stock will be cut 1 inch (3cm) larger than the size of the pages, which will allow a ½-inch (1cm) margin all around. Splitting the difference is easier when using a carpenter's square.

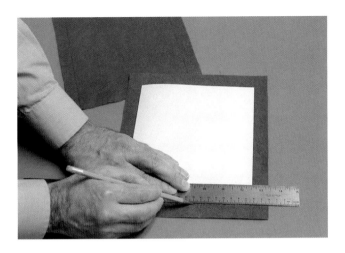

8 Place one of the cut paper pages in the center of the cover. Trace the outline of the page onto the back of the cover with a pencil.

9 Along these lines, pre-crease the folds, doing two opposite sides first.

10 Pre-crease the two other sides.

11 Snip the corners so the layers will not build up when you paste the margins over the inside surfaces.

12 Apply the glue to the folded margins, using a brush.

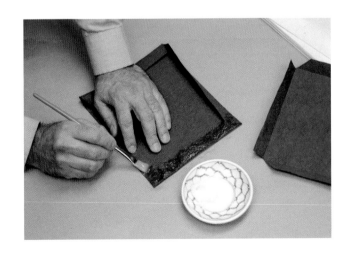

13 Use one folded page as an inside cover. Lay the inside cover surface onto the pasted margins. Repeat this process for the back cover.

14 Press firmly, and then allow it to dry under pressure.

15 Align all the pages and covers, making sure that the folded edges point outward. The folds are your finished edges, and will not be bound.

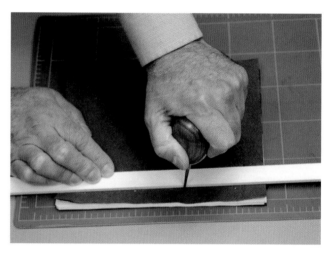

16 Use an awl to punch holes where you will be stitching the binding. Refer to the diagrams at right for the hole placement and sewing method.

Now follow steps 1 through 16, shown on the facing page, in the sewing method for the washi book.

17 This is a view of the sewing method for binding your book as shown in steps 1–5 on the facing page.

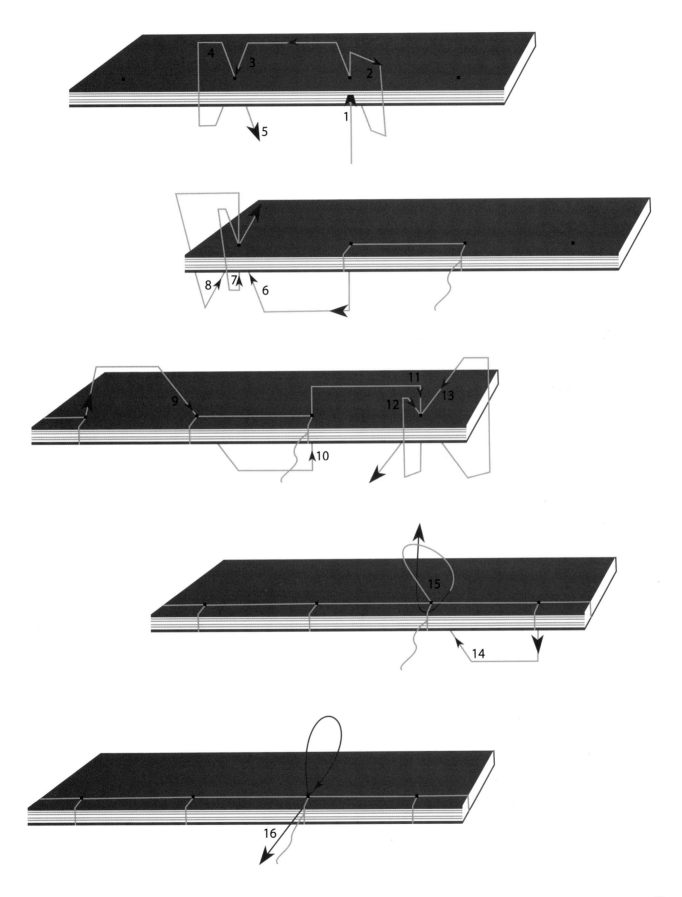

18 This is a view of the sewing method for binding your book after completing step 16 shown in the diagram.

19 Pull the thread tight.

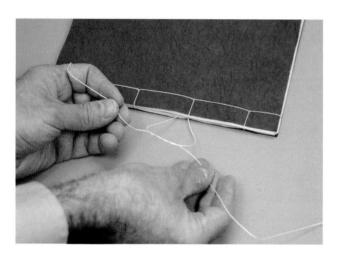

20 Tie off the two ends of the thread, hiding the knot inside the binding.

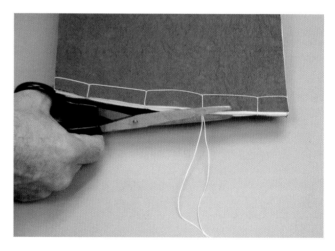

21 Cut off the excess thread after the knot has been tied.

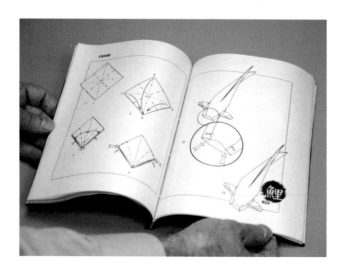

22 Here is the finished Sewn-Bound Washi Book!

All Japan Handmade Washi Association. *Handbook on the Art of Washi*. Tokyo: Wagami-do, K.K., 1991.

Araki, Makio. *Nihon no Orikata Shuu* [A Collection of Japanese Folding Methods]. Kyoto: Tankousha, 1995.

Barrett, Timothy. *Japanese Papermaking: Traditions, Tools, Techniques*. New York: Weatherhill Inc., 1992.

Farnsworth, Donald. *Momigami*. Oakland, CA: Magnolia Editions, Inc., 1997.

Hughes, Sukey. *Washi, The World of Japanese Paper*. New York, Tokyo: Kodansha International, 1978.

Hunter, Dard. *Papermaking: The History and Technique of an Ancient Craft*. New York: Alfred A. Knopf, 1943. Reprint, New York: Dover Publications, Inc., 1978.

Keeton, William T. *Biological Science*. New York: W. W. Norton & Co., 1967.

LaFosse, Michael G. *Advanced Origami: An Artist's Guide to Performances in Paper*. Rutland, VT: Tuttle Publishing, 2005.

LaFosse, Michael G. *Paper Art: The Art of Sculpting with Paper*. Gloucester, MA: Rockport Publishers, Inc., 1998.

Carriage House Paper
79 Guernsey Street, Brooklyn, NY 11222
Donna Koretsky
www.carriagehousepaper.com

Carriage House Paper Museum and Research Institute of Paper History & Technology
8 Evans Road, Brookline, MA 02445
Elaine Koretsky
www.papermakinghistory.org

Dieu Donne Papermill
315 West 36th Street, New York, NY 10018
www.dieudonne.org

The Friends of Dard Hunter, Inc.
P.O. Box 773, Lake Oswego, OR 97034
www.friendsofdardhunter.org

Origami USA
15 West 77th Street, New York, NY 10024
www.origami-usa.org

Origamido Studio
www.origamido.com

SYMBOLS KEY

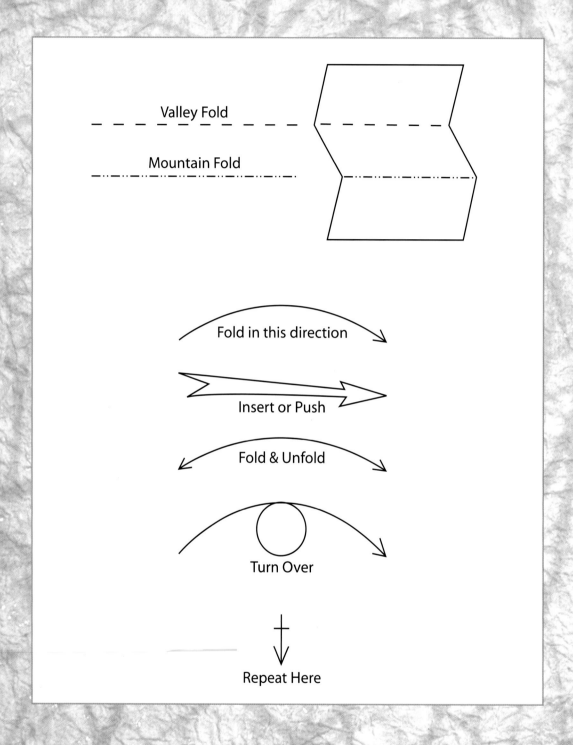

Valley Fold

Mountain Fold

Fold in this direction

Insert or Push

Fold & Unfold

Turn Over

Repeat Here